A Brummie in the Family

Family and Local History in Birmingham

A Brummie in the Family

Family and Local History in Birmingham

Vanessa Morgan

First published 2021

The History Press
97 St George's Place, Cheltenham,
Gloucestershire, GL50 3QB
www.thehistorypress.co.uk

British Library Cataloguing in Publication Data.
A catalogue record for this book is available from the British Library.

ISBN 978 0 7509 9560 3

Typesetting and origination by Typo•glyphix
Printed and bound in Great Britain by TJ Books Limited, Padstow, Cornwall.

Trees for LYfe

Some fifty-odd years ago Dodds, a local comedian, used to sing:

'Brumagen has altered so,
There's scarce a place in it I know
Round the town you now must go
To find old Brumagem.'

Had he lived till these days he might well have sung so, for improvements are being carried out so rapidly now that in another generation it is likely old Birmingham will have been improved off the face of the earth altogether.

Showell's Dictionary of Birmingham (1885)

Old Square. Once found on the corner of Bull Street with Upper and Lower Priory, Old Square was swallowed up by the development of Corporation Street. (Author's Collection)

Contents

Acknowledgements   11

1 Birmingham – a History in its Making   13

2 Researching your Birmingham Roots   38
     The 1939 Register   42
     The Census   44
     Births, Marriages and Deaths   49
     Parish Registers   53
     Bishop's Transcripts   58
     Nonconformist Records   59
     Using the Internet   60
     The Library of Birmingham   61

3 Expanding your Roots   65
     The Parish Chest   65
         Vestry Meeting Minutes   66
         Settlement and Removals   67
         Apprenticeship Indentures   69
         Bastardy Bonds   71
         Overseers' Accounts   72
         Churchwardens' Accounts   73

The Workhouse and the Poor Law Unions 73

Newspapers 75

Court Records 79

Cemeteries 84

Wills and Probates 86

Directories 87

Electoral Registers 88

Land Tax Assessments 89

Hearth Tax 89

Enclosure Awards 90

Tithe Maps and Apportionments 91

School Log Books 92

Rate and Rent Books 93

Manorial Records 94

Military and Police Records 95

4   Compiling and Writing your Family History 98

5   Working in Birmingham 104

6   Life in Birmingham 140

7   Around Birmingham and its Suburbs 184

Aston 187

Saltley 191

Erdington 192

Sutton Coldfield 193

Castle Bromwich 195

Yardley 195

Sheldon 199

Acocks Green 199

Hall Green 200

Balsall Heath 202

Moseley	203
Kings Heath	205
Selly Oak	205
Bournville	206
King's Norton	207
Northfield	208
Edgbaston	209
Harborne	211
Quinton	211
Handsworth	212
Great Barr and Perry Barr	213

Acknowledgements

To tell the story of Birmingham I have found it, in places, more appropriate to use quotes from archival books written many years ago. In that way I am letting the people of the time tell their own story and showing what Birmingham was really like at the time.

One such writer, John Langford, explained in his *A Century of Birmingham Life* that he felt it 'would be more interesting and useful to let our forefathers speak for themselves, than tell their story in other words'. So that is exactly what I have decided to do when describing some of the people and certain parts of the history of Birmingham.

Although there is a large section on 'How to do your Family History', this book is also very much a local history book, which will help you put flesh on the bones of your Brummie ancestors. Hopefully it will show who they were, what they did and how they lived.

So I would like to acknowledge the following that have been invaluable research tools for this book:

History of Birmingham by William Hutton (1783), plus various later editions including the updated version by James Guest, 1836.
A Description of Modern Birmingham by Charles Pye, 1818.
Pigot's Directory, 1841.

Birmingham: History and General Directory of the Borough of Birmingham by Francis White & Co., 1849.

A Century of Birmingham Life (1741–1841) by John Alfred Langford, 1868.

Kelly's Directory, 1872.

Personal Recollections of Birmingham and Birmingham Men, edited from pieces taken from the *Birmingham Daily Mail* signed S.D.R. and published by E. Edwards, 1877.

Showell's Dictionary of Birmingham by Thomas T. Harman and Walter Showell, 1885.

A Tale of One City: The New Birmingham by Thomas Anderton, 1900.

Victoria County History, first published 1901.

I would also like to acknowledge those who contacted me through social media, namely Chris Lea, Ivor Roth, John Sullivan and Peter Jones.

I

Birmingham – a History in its Making

What and who is a Brummie, and where did the name come from?

'Brummie' is an affectionate term used to describe someone who lives in or originated from Birmingham. But why the term Brummie? Throughout time, Birmingham has been recorded with many variations – Brumwycham, Bermyngeham, Bermicham, Bromwycham, Burmyngham, Byrmyngham and Birmingham. But the one name that stuck is Brummagem. This name dates back many centuries and is thought to have derived from a name still being used in the seventeenth century, Bromicham. It should be noted that the word 'Bromwich' is prominent in this part of the Midlands, with other towns such as Castle Bromwich and West Bromwich.

In *A History of Birmingham*, William Hutton tells us that the 'original seems to have been Bromwych: Brom, perhaps, from broom, a shrub, for the growth of which the soil is extremely favourable: Whych, a descent; this exactly corresponds with the declivity from the High Street to Digbeth.' Others say the 'ham', being the Saxon word for home, was then added and therefore translating the name as 'home on the descent on which broom grows'.

However, Charles Pye tells us in *A Century of Birmingham Life*, that 'the derivation of the word Birmingham has been the source of considerable controversy; and has afforded "gentle dullness" one of its favourite occupations.' He also quotes from a piece written in September 1855 by John Freeman in a magazine, the *Athenaeum*:

> The word Birmingham is so thoroughly Saxon in its construction that nothing short of positive historical evidence would warrant us in assigning any other than a Saxon origin to it. The final syllable, ham, means a home or residence, and Bermingas would be a patronymic or family name, meaning the Berms (from Berm, a man's name, and ing or iung, the young, progeny, race, or tribe). The word, dissected in this manner, would signify the home or residence of the Berms; and there can be little question that this is its true meaning.

Other sources refer to the word Brummagen as being a variant to the name, or the way it was said, which appeared locally in the early 1600s. However long ago and how it first started the name has certainly retained its charm right into the twentieth century and beyond as even today Birmingham is still fondly known as Brummagen, or Brum for short.

It may seem incredible now but William Hutton tells us that Birmingham in 1783 was the smallest parish in the district. The largest was King's Norton, being eight times larger than Birmingham. Aston and Sutton were five times larger and Yardley, four times larger. He talked of the springs in Digbeth being so plentiful they could supply the city of London. But in reprinting the book in 1836, James Guest said he was ill-informed, that the springs often dried up and the water from the pumps was hard and not suitable for washing.

From the pages of his book, Hutton takes us on a walk around historic Birmingham as he asks us to:

> perambulate the parish from the bottom of Digbeth, thirty yards north of the bridge. We will proceed south-west up the bed of the old river, with Deritend, in the parish of Aston, on our left. Before we come to the flood-gates, near Vaughton's Hole, we pass by the Longmores, a small part

of King's Norton. Crossing the river Rea, we enter the vestiges of a small rivulet, yet visible, though the stream has been turned, perhaps a thousand years, to supply the moat.

At the top of the first meadow from the river Rea, we meet the little stream above mentioned, in the pursuit of which, we cross the Bromsgrove Road, a little east of the first mile stone. Leaving Banner's Marlpit to the left, we proceed up a narrow lane, crossing the Old Bromsgrove Road, and up the turnpike at Five Ways, in the road to Hales Owen. Leaving this road also to the left, we proceed down the lane, towards Ladywood, cross the Icknield Street, a stone's cast east of the observatory, to the north extremity of Rotton Park, which forms an acute angle, near the Bear at Smethwick.

From the River Rea to this point, is about three miles, rather west, and nearly in a straight line with Edgbaston on the left. We now bear north-east, about a mile, with Smethwick on the left till we meet Shirland Brook, in the Dudley Road; thence to Pigmill. We now leave Handsworth on the left, following the stream through Hockley Great Pool, cross the Wolverhampton Road, and the Icknield Street at the same time down to Aston furnace, with that parish on the left. At the bottom of Walmer Lane we leave the water, move over the fields, nearly in a line to the post by the Peacock, upon Gosty Green.

We now cross the Lichfield Road, down Duke Street, then the Coleshill Road at the A B House. From thence along the meadows to Cooper's Mill; up the river to the foot of Deritend Bridge, and then turn sharp to the right, keeping the course of a drain in the form of a sickle, through John-a-Dean's Hole into Digbeth, from whence we set out.

In marching along Duke Street, we leave about seventy houses to the left, and up the river Rea, about four hundred more in Deritend, reputed part of Birmingham, though not in the parish. This little journey, nearly of an oval form, is about seven miles.

The Francis White *Directory* of 1849 describes Birmingham as:

a Parish, Market Town, and Borough, situated near the centre of the kingdom, in the north western extremity of the County of Warwick, in a sort of peninsula. A small brook, at the distance of about 1½ mile from the centre of the town of Birmingham, separates this county from that of Stafford; and a narrow tongue from the county of Worcester runs into Warwickshire, on the east side of Birmingham. For Ecclesiastical purposes Birmingham is divided into the district parishes of St Martin, St George, St Thomas, and All Saints, in the Archdeaconry of Coventry and Diocese of Worcester.

There seems to be no trace of any prehistoric existence in Birmingham, the suggestion being that the marsh land in the Rea valley would not have attracted any such settlement. When the Romans arrived they set up camp at Metchley in Edgbaston, where the Queen Elizabeth hospital now stands, and built a station on a nearby hill. Named Bremenium, Bre and Maen meaning the high stone, it provided a good view of the surrounding country. Ryknield Street passed to the west of what we now know of as Birmingham, and joined the camp at Metchley with the camp at Wall, near Lichfield. It ran through Hockley into Handsworth and then on to Sutton Park.

Of Ryknield Street Charles Pye wrote:

The old Roman road, denominated Iknield-street, that extends from Southampton to Tynemouth, enters this parish near the observatory in Ladywood-lane, crosses the road to Dudley at the Sand Pits, and proceeding along Warstone-lane, leaves the parish in Hockley-brook; but is distinctly to be seen at the distance of five miles, both in Sutton Park and on the Coldfield, in perfect repair, as when the Romans left it.

The first evidence of the beginnings of a town, or-be-it a village, in these early centuries was in Saxon times. Here a small settlement was established in the scrubland and woods that formed part of the Forest of Arden, which then covered a large area of Warwickshire and parts of Staffordshire between the River Avon and the River Tame. Although no actual documentation exists, it is thought that an officer, who came over during an invasion in AD 582 was given the land as a reward and that it was his family who eventually took the name 'de Bermingham'.

It was Peter de Bermingham who is first recorded as using the name when in 1156 the manor, as it had now become, was granted a market charter by Henry II. For centuries the market was held regularly on a Thursday but with expansion in later centuries additional markets were held on Mondays and Saturdays. In 1251, William de Bermingham acquired a charter from Henry III to hold two fairs in the town; one at Whitsun, commencing on the eve of Holy Thursday and continuing for four days, the other on the eve of St Michael, continuing for three days.

The manor house, home to the 'de Bermingham' family, was known as The Moat and stood close to St Martin's Church just west of Digbeth, with the water supply for the actual moat coming from a small stream fed by the River Rea. This stream flowed from Vaughton's Hole on the border with Edgbaston. Of the moat, William Hutton wrote 'being filled with water,

St Martin's Church and the Bull Ring, early 1900s. Once the centre of medieval Birmingham. (Author's Collection)

it has the same appearance now as perhaps a thousand years ago, but not altogether the same use. It then served to protect its master, but now to turn a thread mill.'

The manor house is known to have existed at the time of the Domesday Book but how far back it went before then is not known. However, in the 1960s excavations were carried out in order to build a new ring road and it was discovered that the entrance seemed to point away from what was the town centre in medieval times, suggesting the building was there before the town had developed around the market. Maps of the 1700s for the area show that all medieval buildings had gone and then in the early 1800s The Moat was also demolished to provide space for a new market.

By 1538 Birmingham had a population of 1,500. It was made up of one main street, a few side streets and 200 houses. However, the manor was now no longer owned by the de Bermingham family.

Edward Bermingham was born in 1497 and, because his father had died, succeeded his grandfather at the age of 3. A ward-ship was granted by Henry VII to Lord Edward Dudley but by the time the young Edward was old enough to take charge of the manor, the Dudley family had become ambitious. John Dudley, 1st Duke of Northumberland, wanted the manor for himself and offered to buy it but Edward refused. Determined to have it, Dudley hatched a dastardly plan. He arranged for some men to be on the road at the same time as Edward, then having met him to strike up a conversation with him and to continue to ride with him. Further up the road another man would be waiting for them. The plan fell into place and when Edward arrived at the designated spot his new companions drew their guns and robbed their waiting accomplice. Keeping up the pretence, the man reported the robbery and Edward, being highly recognisable, was arrested. The other men, of course, were never found so Edward, despite protesting his innocence was tried, found guilty and sentenced to death. His lands were confiscated by the King and Dudley was then able to acquire them for himself. However, he did arrange for Edward to be pardoned and he was given an income of £40 a year in compensation for the loss of property.

William Hutton tells us that the place the robbery took place was Sandy Lane in Aston.

Afterwards the Bermingham family seem to fall into obscurity, except William Hutton does say that he once met a man who had the name Birmingham and 'was pleased with the hope of finding a member of that ancient and honourable house; but he proved so amazingly ignorant, he could not tell whether he was from the clouds, the seas, or the dunghill; instead of tracing the existance of his ancestors, even so high as his father, he was scarcely conscious of his own.'

However, in this modern age, a search on various family history sites bring up a lot of people in Birmingham with the name Birmingham in various genealogy records. Perhaps someone has done their family history and has found they are descended from this illustrious family. Or perhaps you will.

In the 1500s Birmingham was growing and had a successful industry in the weaving and dyeing of wool, and the making of leather goods. But also a new industry, which was to shape the future of Birmingham, was established. With the natural resources of iron ore, coal and streams, many forges and water mills were being set up where knives and nails could be made. The iron ore provided the necessary material for these items, the coal and the streams provided the fuel needed to power to the forges.

Between 1538 and 1543 John Leland, a poet and antiquary, travelled through England making observations, which he sent to Henry VIII. Of Birmingham he wrote, as reprinted in Francis White's *Directory* of 1849,

I came through a pretty street as ever I entered, into Birmingham town. This street, as I remember, is called Dirtey (Deritend). In it dwell smiths and cutlers, and there is a brook that divides this street from Birmingham, an hamlet member belonging to the parish thereby. There is at the end of Dirtey a proper chapel, and mansion house of timber (the moat) hard on the ripe (bank) as the brook runneth down, and I went through the ford by the bridge, the water came down on the right hand, and a few miles below goeth into the Tame. This brook, above Dirtey, breaketh into two arms; that a little beneath the bridge close again. This brook riseth, as some say, four or five miles above Birmingham, towards black hills. The beauty of Birmingham, a good market town in the extreme parts of Warwickshire, is one street going up alonge, almost from the left ripe of the brook, up a mean hill, by the length of a quarter of a mile. I saw but one parish church in the town. A great part of is maintained by smithes, who have their iron and sea-coal out of Staffordshire.

The oldest building in Birmingham is undoubtedly the Old Crown Inn, having been standing on the High Street in Deritend since 1368, and it seems the same family owned it for many years as *Showell's Dictionary* tells of a Mr Toulmin Smith, 'in whose family the Old Crown House has descended from the time it was built'. The writer goes on to say that it was thought Deritend was originally known as Deer-Gate-End but that 'Leland said he entered the town by Dirtey, so perhaps after all Deritend only means 'the dirty end'. 'We are also told that Digbeth was known as Dyke Path, or Dicks' Bath, and was another puzzle to the antiquarians, 'It was evidently a watery place, and the pathway lay low.'

It does not seem that Birmingham became too involved in the Civil War, although it is listed as being a parliamentary town. However, the Battle of Birmingham did take place on 3 April 1643 around Camp Hill when a company of Cromwell's men from a garrison in Lichfield, together with some local men, tried to prevent a Royalist detachment led by Prince Rupert from entering the town. Prince Rupert's battalion of foot soldiers and cavalry killed a number of inhabitants and burnt around eighty houses, causing damage amounting to £30,000. Then, at the end of that year, Parliamentary soldiers, again with the help of some townsmen, captured Aston Hall.

By the end of the 1600s the population of Birmingham amounted to 4,000 and an anonymous writer, whose comments were published in *Showell's Dictionary of Birmingham*, wrote in 1691 that:

Bromichan drives a good trade in iron and steel wares, saddles and bridles. A large and well-built town, very populous, much resorted to, and particularly noted a few years ago for the counterfeit groats made here, and dispersed all over the kingdom.

In 1731 another anonymous writer spoke of the people of Birmingham being – 'mostly smiths, and very ingenious in their way, and vend vast quantities of all sorts of iron wares'.

In 1766 *A New Tour through England*, written by George Beaumont and Capt Harry Disney, describes Birmingham as:

a very populous town, the upper part of which stands dry on the side of a hill, but the lower is watry, and inhabited by the meaner sort of people. They are employed here in the Iron Works, in which they are such ingenious artificers, that their performances in the smallwares of iron and steel are admired both at home and abroad.

The *London Chronicle* wrote in August 1788 of a gentleman who visited Birmingham and said. 'The people are all diminutive in size, sickly in appearance, and spend their Sundays in low debauchery.' Of the manufacturers he noted that there was 'a great deal of trick and low cunning as well as profligacy'.

During the 1700s those small but 'ingenious' people in Birmingham had doubled in size. In 1720 the population had risen to almost 12,000. Thirty years later that figure had doubled. By the end of that century it had risen to 73,000, with a census in 1801 giving a population of 73,670. Industry was also booming. Metal workers were producing numerous items including shoe buckles, buttons, pens, knives and bolts. Brass was also popular, as was gun making.

It was during the 1700s that industry took an important role in the development of Birmingham and one man who played a major role in this was Matthew Boulton and his innovation, which was the Soho Works.

Soho was just a barren heath between Birmingham and Handsworth but in 1756 Edward Rushton leased a piece of land, deepened Hockley Brook and built a small mill. Eight years later Boulton purchased the lease from

Soho House. The home of Matthew Boulton, now a museum celebrating his life and work. Bought in 1766 when just a farmhouse, Boulton spent many years renovating it into a gentleman's mansion typical of the Georgian era. (Author's Photograph)

him and the site was transformed. A directory of 1774, an extract of which was published in *Showell's Dictionary*, described the works as consisting of 'four squares of buildings, with workshops, &c., for more than a thousand workmen'. Soho House, the home Boulton bought for himself in order to be on the doorstep of his works, was host to many celebrities of the day; inventors rubbing shoulders with lords and ladies, students with philosophers and such-like.

Up until this time the roads around Birmingham had not been good. In 1659 it took four days to get from London to Birmingham, but this had improved by 1747 and coaches were advertising that the journey could be done in two days. With the lack of a navigable river and roads of poor quality, the development of Birmingham had been slow but the river did have its uses, as Charles Pye writes:

The only stream of water that flows to this town is a small rivulet, denominated the river Rea, which takes its rise upon Rubery Hill, near one mile north of Bromsgrove Lickey, about eight miles distant, from whence there being a considerable descent, numerous reservoirs have been made, which enables the stream, within that short space, to drive ten mills, exclusive of two within the town; and what is very remarkable, some person has erected a windmill very near its banks, where the ground is not in the least elevated. The curiosity of a windmill being erected in a valley, is very visible soon after you have passed the buildings on the road to Bromsgrove.

After leaving its source the River Rea travels through Rubery and Longbridge, and after travelling through an underground culvert, reaches Northfield. From there it runs through Stirchley, Cannon Hill Park, Balsall Heath to Digbeth. Stretching 14 miles, it joins the River Tame at Gravelly Hill.

It was the development of the canal system that helped in the expansion of Birmingham and its industry. An act in 1767 saw the building of a canal between Birmingham and the collieries near Wolverhampton and Wednesbury, meaning the easier distribution of coal, which had previously been transported by land. Following the opening of the canal, there was an immediate reduction in the price of coal. Eventually the canal was extended to reach the Staffordshire canal.

Charles Pye wrote of the canal system in 1812:

In the year 1767 an act of parliament was obtained to cut a canal from this town to the collieries, which was completed in 1769, at the expense of £70,000. There is now a regular communication by water between this town, London, Liverpool, Manchester and Bristol; to the three former places, goods are delivered on the fourth day, upon a certainty; there being relays of horses stationed every fifteen minutes.

The *Dictionary of Birmingham* tells us that on 6 November 1769 the first boat-load of coal arrived in Birmingham from Bilston and was 'hailed as one of the greatest blessings that could be conferred on the town'.

In 1793 the cutting of the Warwick canal began and Pye wrote:

The Warwick Canal was opened for the passage of boats, by forming a junction with the Birmingham canal by means of which goods may be conveyed from the upper part of this town, to London, one whole day sooner than they can by steering immediately into the Warwick canal. At King's-Norton, this canal is conveyed under ground, by means of a tunnel, two miles in length, which is in width 16 feet and in height 18 feet, yet it is so admirably constructed, that any person by looking in at one end, may perceive day-light at the other extremity.

There was a price to pay for the convenience as a small charge was made per tonnage. But most thought it was worth it in order to save a day's travel. And going along the new route boatmen also avoided twelve locks that could cause wear and tear on their boats.

During the first week in January 1800 newspapers reported the opening of this new canal, plus another:

At 12 o'clock on Thursday, a boat, loaded upwards of 20 tons of coal, navigated along the Warwick and Birmingham canal, and a boat, loaded with 100 qrs. of lime, navigated along the Warwick and Napton canal, met at the junction of the two canals, at Warwick; their arrival was announced by the firing of cannon and ringing of bells, and received with the loudest acclamations by a great concourse of spectators, assembled on the occasion. A wagon, loaded with coals from the boat, was drawn through the town by men, attended by several of the canal proprietors, several inhabitants of the place, and more than 600 men who had been employed in the works, walked in procession, with a band of music, flag flying, &c. The opening of these canals will be a vast advantage to the trade of Birmingham with the metropolis. Goods sent by water, via Warwick and Oxford, will have 41 mile less to go than by any other navigation.

The canals were a great asset to Birmingham industry as Charles Pye continues:

the trade of this town has within the last fifteen years increased in an astonishing manner, for in the year 1803, six weekly boats were sufficient to convey all the merchandize to and from this town to Manchester and Liverpool but at the present time, there are at least twenty boats weekly employed in that trade.

Other canals joined the system around Birmingham, which provided a link not only with Dudley, Stourbridge, Fazeley, Coventry and Warwick but further afield to Oxford, Manchester and Liverpool. However, the building of the canal system was no easy task for the canal engineers. The steep inclines and slopes around Birmingham meant an abundance of locks. The canal to Wednesbury had to be built up a hill, which meant the construction of six locks. It took twenty-four years to build the Worcester to Birmingham canal.

So Birmingham, once cut off through having no navigable river in its vicinity, was now accessible to the rest of the country with an abundance of waterways and as described by Charles Pye: 'Notwithstanding there is only one stream of water, the streets are so intersected by canals, that there is only one entrance into the town without coming over a bridge, and that is from Worcester.'

Birmingham may have avoided any involvement in the Civil War but in the space of just under fifty years it was to witness two vicious assaults on some of its residents and property.

In 1791, with the French revolution still in the minds of people, many were becoming suspicious of those who had become dissenters, in particular their head, Joseph Priestley. So when a notice appeared in the newspapers inviting 'like-minded people' to a dinner at the Dadley Hotel on Temple Row suspicions were raised. The dinner for eighty-one guests took place on Thursday, 14 July at 3 o'clock, and while the guests dined a mob gathered outside. It started quite peaceable with jeering and booing but then someone supposedly heard a toast being made of 'destruction to the present government and the King's head upon a charger'. What followed was a weekend of terror.

The mob rushed into the hotel, breaking windows and furniture and as the diners tried to make their exit they were pelted with stones. From there some of the mob went to Priestley's meeting house and set fire to it, while others went to his house at Fair Hill and set fire to that – although not before looting his cellar and becoming intoxicated on his wines. As more joined the mob, other houses suffered the same fate: John Ryland's house on Easy Hill; John Taylor's property, Moseley Hall; William Hutton's house on Bennetts Hill and many more all over the town, including other meeting houses. All the time the rioters were chanting, 'Long live the King, Church and State. Down with dissenters.' Soldiers came from both Oxford and Nottingham but it took all weekend to dispel the rioters. Many scattered and avoided arrest. Of those who were arrested, only two were hanged for their so-called crimes: Francis Field and John Green. Others miraculously found themselves alibis.

The Chartist Riots took place in the summer of 1839. There had been a large number of Chartist meetings all over the country and on 1 July they started assembling in the Bull Ring in Birmingham. The police tried to move them on but were attacked with the flag poles the crowd were carrying. Soldiers arrived to help and forced the crowd down Digbeth and eventually to St Thomas' Church. Here the mob pulled out the iron palisades from around the church and used them as weapons. On this occasion they were eventually dispersed but two weeks later another meeting was organised that was to take place at Holloway Head and 2,000 people assembled. At first it was very peaceful but when it ended large groups went on the rampage. Rushing down to the Bull Ring and the streets of Deritend, they threw stones at windows and broke iron palisades to use as weapons. They ransacked shops and made bonfires of the contents they had dragged from the buildings. Furniture was destroyed and goods from the shelves were piled high on the bonfires, in fact anything that could be burned was thrown on to the fires. Eventually the military arrived to assist the police and the mob fled. Thirty people were arrested. Four were eventually executed, while others were sentenced to transportation for varying periods.

It would be another hundred years before Birmingham saw devastation such as this and by then it would have grown and developed at an alarming rate, once again all down to a new transport system.

In the 1800s the canals around Birmingham were becoming so populated they were at times too overcrowded and so thoughts quickly turned to the new mode of transport – the railway.

As early as 1824 a suggestion had been made in parliament regarding the building of a railway in Birmingham, but it had been refused. Six years later another survey was drawn up for a line to be built between Birmingham and London. Eventually the act was passed and the work began in June 1834. It took four years to complete and by September 1838 passengers could travel not only to London but locally to Coventry and Rugby, too.

At first there were two separate companies – the London & Birmingham Railway Company and the Grand Junction Railway Company. Both had their stations side-by-side in Curzon Street. Then in 1846 they merged to become the London and North Western Railway, taking passengers to Manchester and Liverpool, and locally to Walsall and Wolverhampton. When other lines were completed, passengers could travel to Bristol and the West Country or north to Derby, Sheffield, Newcastle upon Tyne and then on to Scotland.

There were other railway stations in Duddeston Row, Lawley Street, Vauxhall and Camp Hill, but it was soon realised that a central station was necessary and New Street was the chosen spot. Work to clear the area began in 1846 and *Showell's Dictionary of Birmingham* tells us that 'several streets were done away with, and the introduction of the station may be called the date-point of the many town improvements that have since been carried out. The station, and the tunnels leading thereto, took seven years in completion, the opening ceremony taking place June 1, 1853.'

There was no grand opening, just a low-key ceremony as passengers had actually been able to use the station since 1851.

The coming of the railways were not only good for the economy of Birmingham but also for its well-being. In 1900 Thomas Anderton wrote of the squalor of the previous thirty years and that these improvements had been slow, with the powers-that-be too careful and economical to make any changes. However, he also wrote that:

> the construction of the London and North Western Railway station cleared away a large area of slums that were scarcely fit for those who lived in them. A region sacred to squalor and low drinking shops, a paradise of marine store dealers, a hotbed of filthy courts tenanted by a low and degraded class, was swept away to make room for the large station. The Great Western Railway station, too, in its making also disposed of some shabby, narrow streets and dirty, pestiferous houses inhabited by people who were not creditable to the locality or the community, and by so doing contributed to the improvement of the town.

Birmingham now saw an even larger opening for its commercial businesses with a quicker turnover in the movement of both the raw materials it needed for its factories and its ability to pass on the finished product to its customers. All this needed more workers and so the population increased as workers arrived from other parts of the neighbouring counties and even farther afield. This saw the need for more public buildings.

The Public Office and prison had been built on Moor Street in 1805 and contained the offices for the Street Commissioners as well as the magistrates' court but by 1830 it needed to be enlarged. Thirty years later, in 1861, it was enlarged again.

The original prison in Peck Lane had opened in 1697 and was extended in 1757. In *Showell's Dictionary of Birmingham* we read that:

> A writer, in 1802, described it as a shocking place, the establishment consisted of one day room, two underground dungeons (in which sometimes

half-a-dozen persons had to sleep), and six or seven night rooms some of them constructed out of the Gaoler's stables. The prisoners were allowed 4d per day for bread and cheese, which they had to buy from the keeper. In 1806 a new gaol was built at the back of the Public Office in Moor Street which consisted of two day rooms, sixteen cells and a courtyard.

The new gaol was built to avoid the gathering of crowds who came out to watch the prisoners travelling between Peck Lane and the Public Office. It was only used as a temporary holding place while the prisoner was being held in custody. Once they had been charged by the magistrates, in most cases, they were sent to Warwick gaol to await their trial at the assizes. When the Victoria Law Courts were opened in 1891 the Moor Street site was eventually developed into a railway station and the lock-up was moved to Steelhouse Lane, where a tunnel under Coleridge Passage was used to move prisoners between the cells and the court.

For petty crimes, punishment could be a session in the stocks. The stocks were situated in the yard at the Public Office. Prior to 1806 they were at Welch Cross, at the junction of Bull Street, High Street and Dale End.

Previously the office for the Justices of the Peace was situated in Dale End and a prison on the High Street in Bordesley. In 1802 this prison was classed as the worst gaol in England as *Showell's* tells us that:

the prison was in the backyard of the keeper's house, and it comprised two dark, damp dungeons, twelve feet by seven feet, to which access was gained through a trapdoor, level with the yard and down ten steps. The only light or air that could reach these cells (which sometimes were an inch deep in water) was through a single iron-grated aperture about a foot square. For petty offenders, runaway apprentices, and disobedient servants, there were two other rooms, opening into the yard, each about twelve feet square.

The use of the underground rooms was discontinued in 1809.

The imposing and austere Victoria Law Courts *c.* 1900. (Author's Collection)

The old Debtors' Prison was in Philip Street in a small courtyard and consisted of one dirty damp room, 10ft by 11ft at the bottom of seven steps. Sometimes this room held fifteen people at one time, male and female. This was also closed in 1809 with the building of the new Public Office.

As Birmingham was part of Warwickshire, the majority of criminals were taken to Warwick Gaol and tried at the Warwick Assizes. It was not until the 1840s that Winson Green Prison was built.

Built between 1845 and 1849, Winson Green Prison contained 321 cells for both men and women. When it opened on 29 October 1849 it was known as the Gaol at Birmingham Heath. In 1885 it became a hanging prison for those convicted at the Birmingham Assizes. The first man hanged there was Henry Kimberley for the murder of Emma Palmer.

The foundation stone for the Victoria Law Courts was laid by Queen Victoria on 23 March 1887. She arrived at Small Heath station at about 1 o'clock, from where a small procession of soldiers, police and firemen accompanied the two carriages which carried her and her entourage to the

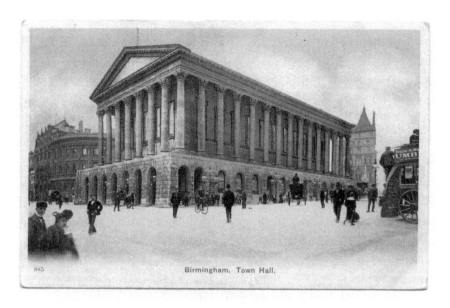

The Town Hall in earlier times but still an important building today. (Author's Collection)

Town Hall. The streets were crowded and she arrived at the Town Hall just after 2 o'clock to a fanfare of trumpets. After a short musical presentation, the Queen had a private lunch. Afterwards the procession took her to Corporation Street, where the first stone lay waiting. She tapped the stone three times with an ivory mallet and then left for Snow Hill station and her return to Windsor.

The Triennial Music Festival, which was originally established to raise funds for the building of the hospital, had been held since 1784 in St Philip's Church. By the 1820s the church had become too small to hold the number of people who wanted to attend the concerts, so it was necessary to build a larger building. Work on the new Town Hall began in 1828 with an estimated cost of between £17,000 and £19,000. However by the time it was eventually completed in 1850, with many alterations being made over the years, it had cost £69,520. It was described in *Showell's Dictionary* as being a 'most conspicuous building, as well as the finest specimen of architecture, in the town.' The building included a 6,000-pipe organ.

When it opened in 1834 it was claimed to be the finest music hall in the country and over the years many famous people have appeared there and many events have taken place, including wrestling matches and a Rolling Stones concert. But in the early days it was people such as Charles Dickens, reading *A Christmas Carol*, who attracted the crowds. Since then many prime ministers have spoken there and a variety of music has been heard, from classical to jazz. Many premiers have taken place: Mendelssohn's *Elijah*, Elgar's *The Dream of Gerontius* and Sir Arthur Sullivan's *Overture di Ballo*. Throughout the 1960s and '70s many great rock bands made the Town Hall their venue when visiting Birmingham. In 1996 it closed for refurbishment but reopened in 2007 with a two-week festival celebrating both the past and the future. The original organ had also been renovated.

In 1883 Lincoln's Inn was built in Corporation Street, opposite the county court, at a cost of £22,000. Like its London namesake, it was intended to house firms of solicitors, accountants, and such-like. *Showell's* writes of it:

> The outside appearance of the block is very striking, having a large entrance gateway with a circular bay window over it, surmounted by a lofty tower. The tower has four clock faces, pinnacles at the angles, and a steep slate roof, and is 120 feet high. There are also two flanking towers, at the extreme ends of the front. These have canted bay windows below them, and their pediments are surmounted by figures representing Mercury and Athaene. The space on each side between the central and the flanking tower is divided into three bays, having ornamental dormers above them, and being divided by niches, which will serve to hold allegorical figures of art. The windows are ornamented by tracery, and the facade is enriched by a free use of carving.

The county court on the corner of Corporation Street and Newton Street was built for a cost of £20,000 around the time *Showell's Dictionary* was being published. But it seems *Showell* did not like this new building as he wrote, 'built of Hollington Stone, in Italian style, though, like that other Government-built edifice, the new Post Office, it is of too heavy an appearance'.

Gas lighting seems to have arrived in Birmingham during the late 1700s to early 1800s. The first to install these lights was the Soho Works around 1798 and according to newspapers in 1802 there was certainly an exhibition of the lights during that year.

The instigator of this new venture was William Murdoch, who had moved to Birmingham to work with Boulton and Watt in the Soho steam business in 1777. During the ensuing years he also spent time in Cornwall, where he maintained the engines used to pump the water out of the tin mines. As a boy he had discovered that by putting coal dust in his mother's old kettle he could set fire to the steam coming out. Using this method Murdoch constructed a light system in his house in Redruth. Hearing of this new invention, Boulton and Watt asked him to develop similar lighting for their Soho works. At first two gas lamps were installed but before long the whole factory was lit by gas.

At first it seems the lighting was only used by factories. Among them was Jones, Smart & Co., which had 120 burners installed to light their glassworks. However, some improvised with the equipment they already had. Benjamin Cook in Caroline Street fitted his premises in 1808 using old or waste gun barrels for his pipes.

Gas street lighting was proposed in 1811 and although one or two private companies set the odd lamp around the streets, it was not until 1826 that the principal streets in Birmingham were illuminated. The Birmingham Gas Company was formed in 1817 but was limited to laying their pipes only in Birmingham. Then in 1825 the Birmingham and Staffordshire Gas Company was formed in West Bromwich with the works being built in Adderley Street that serviced a large area of Birmingham.

Newspapers reported, 'We have satisfaction to inform our readers, that the Birmingham and Staffordshire Gas Company have nearly completed their great undertaking for lighting the town with gas, and that it is expected, that many of the street lamps will be lighted this week.' However it seems most people could not understand what gas was and how it would flow from West Bromwich to Birmingham through the pipes. So the company undertook an experiment and said that 'a pressure of air equal 1.95 inch of water being admitted into the said pipes, at eleven o'clock A.M. the effect was observed in Birmingham by the workmen about three minutes past eleven A.M..'

The two companies did not try to undercut one another and worked happily side-by-side for fifty years. Then in 1874 Joseph Chamberlain proposed to purchase both companies on behalf of the Borough and they became known as the Municipal Gas Scheme. In its first year the company made a profit of £34,000.

White's *Directory* tells us that Birmingham had an ample supply of clean water in the wells around the town until the numbers in the population increased. With new homes being built and the increasing number of factories springing up, all adding to problems with pollution, the wells became insufficient. An act to set up the Water Works Company was passed in 1825 and shares were immediately issued in order to build the waterworks. The works took six years to complete but were ready to start delivering water in 1831.

Nelson's Monument, looking across the Bull Ring to St Martin's Church. (Author's Collection)

Built in Aston, on the Lichfield Road, the water supply was taken from the River Tame and a brook near Salford Bridge. There were two reservoirs; 'the main one being in Aston where two steam engines were used to push the water through the pipes. A second reservoir was built in Edgbaston and it was said that both reservoirs held enough water to last eight or ten weeks. The first house to be supplied with water, in March 1831, was the home of Mr H. Meriden in St Paul's Square.

The Municipal Corporations Act of 1835 provided towns and cities with their own councils rather than belonging to a larger borough. Those elected would be responsible for only a small area each as it was felt that previously certain areas had been neglected by those in power.

The Street Commissioners were replaced, although the replacement was gradual. Originally introduced in 1769, their job was to keep the streets clean, regulate the traffic and look after the watchmen. Later they had been tasked to improve specifically chosen areas. They had provided new roads, paved streets and arranged markets. In 1801, with a budget of £1,730, they had set about making improvements around the Bull Ring. Nine tenements were removed and the area cleared into a central open space. Five years later the remaining houses and shops had been purchased around St Martin's to make further improvements.

Also included in the demolition was the Old Cross. Also known as Market Cross, this was a building raised up on arches, which gave shelter underneath to the market traders and at one time was considered to be the central point of Birmingham. After its removal the centre spot became known as Nelson's Monument, which stands between St Martin's and the Bull Ring.

In 1885 *Showell's Dictionary of Birmingham* tells us that at that time the centre of Birmingham was considered to be Attwood's statue at the top of Stephenson's Place, in New Street. But it added that in the authors' opinion 'so far as the irregular shape of the borough area will allow of such measurement being made, the central spot is covered by Messrs. Marris and Norton's warehouse in Corporation Street'. This building is still there, on the corner of Fore Street. However, today it seems the centre of Birmingham is just classed as being within the Inner Ring Road.

It took three years to establish the new corporation and an election for the first town council took place on 26 December 1838. The town was divided into thirteen wards, and sixteen alderman and forty-eight councillors were elected. William Scolefield became the first Mayor and William Redfern was appointed as Town Clerk.

Showell also wrote of the future of Birmingham, saying:

It has been proposed that the Borough should be extended so as to include the Local Board districts of Harborne and Handsworth, Balsall Heath, Moseley, King's Heath, part of King's Norton parish, the whole of Yardley and Acocks Green, Saltley, Witton, Little Bromwich, and Erdington covering an area of about 32,000 acres, with a present population of over half a million.

Birmingham had certainly grown by the 1880s and now this town, once a village, once a market town and then an industrial town had become more important, and so in 1889 it was given a city status by Queen Victoria. On Friday, 30 November 1888 the *Birmingham Daily Post* wrote that:

We announce this morning a little surprise for the Town Council in the first place, and for the town in the second. Without anybody knowing anything about it, an arrangement has been quietly matured by which Birmingham is to undergo a sort of transformation. It will keep its name – that is a comfort – but it is to change its condition, and to assume a different corporate status. Within the memory of people now living our popular name, much cherished by Birmingham men of that day, was that of 'Hardware Village'. Then we were legally a town, a community taking the name of the ancient parish. Fifty years ago we were made into a borough, and when that alteration of title was conferred we absorbed another parish and part of a third. Having been a borough for just half a century, we are now to be converted into a city: that is, we shall be, if we ask for it – these distinctions, it seems, being granted only on request.

The report then goes on to say that on 31 October 1838 Birmingham was given the Charter of Incorporation, so it had been decided, with the occasion of the fiftieth anniversary coming up, to write to the Home Secretary to ask if 'her Majesty might be willing, on such an occasion, to confer the title of city upon the town'.

The majority felt that Birmingham should now be a city, but there were some who questioned it. However, as the newspaper report said:

> many visitors, especially those from foreign parts, have usually insisted upon calling the place a city. But though in substance there will be no change, in sentiment there will be. Borough and burgesses are good, solid, homely English words, and we shall part from them with regret; but city and citizens are names that link us with a greater and grander past, which convey a fuller and deeper meaning, and which, while implying a higher sense of dignity, impose also upon those who bear them an obligation to a still worthier and larger communal life. So we think the Town Council will do well to ask the Queen to make Birmingham a city.

Permission was granted and Birmingham became a city in January 1889.

And so Birmingham continued its growth and prosperity through into the nineteenth century. It expanded its boundaries and took parts of the surrounding parishes into its jurisdiction. It lost its young men in the First World War and then again in the Second. The bombings of the Second World War took many of its buildings but once again it, and its people, took the devastation in their stride and rebuilt. Old industries disappeared, new ones appeared. Now in the twenty-first century there is a new look to Birmingham and one day these new buildings will be the old buildings just as the manor house of the de Bermingham family became and people will be looking back at us with interest.

2

Researching your Birmingham Roots

So, you want to find out all about your ancestors. To become involved in a hobby that is now probably one of the most popular pastimes of modern times. But where do you start? Probably the most obvious place is with your own family. Talk to them, ask them questions. But while the older members will have more knowledge of family from many years ago, beware of 'Chinese whispers'. Great Aunt Mabel may say, 'My grandma told me we were related to …' But in actual fact her grandma had only said, 'I wonder if we're related to …' Regardless of this, still make a note of everything you are told. You can always dismiss it later.

There are so many questions to ask and you will probably know yourself what you feel you would like to know, but here are a few suggestions to give you an idea.

When and where were you born and how did your parents come to live there? When were they born, when were their parents born? Can you remember the years any deceased relations died and how old they were? Where did family members live? These questions are important in getting an idea of the time frame of what years you will need to cover, and where, when you make a start. To get a background into their lives you could also ask – did other family members live nearby? Which older relatives do you remember when you were growing up? What stories were you told about any who died before you were born. Where did other members of your family live and what were their houses like, had they lived there a long time? Was anyone in the family involved in an historic event?

Of course you can elaborate on your family history, to tell a story that future generations will enjoy, by asking questions other than those that just relate to genealogy. Questions about their school life, their friends, what they did for pleasure, the holidays they went on and days out. When they left school, where was their first job, did they like it? What did they do for hobbies, did they play any sports? What were the happiest times of their lives? But sometimes you might not need to ask all these questions. Once they start talking all these stories will probably be covered during the course of the conversation.

Make sure you always ask to see any certificates or other old documents they have. If they don't want to part with them in this day and age it is easy enough to take a photo on your phone. Or you can do it the old-fashioned way – write it all down. Someone's death certificate will show their age when they died, so immediately you can work out when they were born. A birth certificate will immediately give you another generation when you see the names of the parents, including the mother's maiden name. Likewise, a marriage certificate will give you another generation, albeit only the fathers' names. But the witness who signed the certificate may be of use at a later date when you find other members of the family. If one of those witnesses turns out to be a sibling or a cousin it can be extra proof that you have found the correct piece of the puzzle.

Do they have any old photographs? Something might be scribbled on the back, which is really useful. But it is always nice to see what old members of the family looked like, putting a face to a name, to see what they are wearing and such-like.

When you first start going through old records you may be confused by the spellings of a name. You will find that names are spelt very differently, not only from how they are now, but on each register or record you look at. With so many people being illiterate in the times of our ancestors, spelling was not that important. An official would spell a name how he heard it. Even down to the 'dropped-H'. Harris can sometimes be seen as Arris and Haines as Ainge – not just the dropped H here but a strong accent making the N sound like a G. The larger cities such as Birmingham are often the worst cases for these spelling discrepancies. With people moving to the towns from the surrounding countryside looking for work there would have been a great variety of strong accents the officials may not really have heard before.

Nicknames can also confuse things. Your mother might have often referred to her uncle Jim. So quite rightly you would assume his name was James. But was that his first name? You search frantically for him among all the James, then someone just happens to say, 'Oh James was his middle name.' A middle name was regularly used by people and there he is listed as William James. It works the other way, too. You might have a birth certificate for a William James and you're trying to find him in the census. Eventually you find him and realise the name he gave the enumerator was his commonly used name of Jim and not his full name. That was another trait our ancestors had. They did not always realise they should be using their full and proper names when filling in government forms or such-like.

So you are now ready to start but first there is one more thing to remember before you do: remember to keep methodical records of where and what you have searched. Draw up a research plan and learn about the records you are searching and if they are not a digitised version of the original, go to the library to look at the original, or arrange for someone to get you a copy.

Another warning as you progress. You will soon learn that our ancestors had a habit of telling lies; anything from little white lies to huge great porkies. You find this more in the labouring families who were suspicious of the authorities knowing too much about them. For example, when giving their details for the census they often added or subtracted years on their age. Sometimes they changed the place of their birth.

To be fair to our ancestors though, it was not always untruths, sometimes they genuinely didn't know. If they were born before 1837, the year official certificates came into existence, they would have no birth certificate to jog their memory. And although birthday celebrations were introduced by the

Victorians, it was really only for the wealthy so, again, with the labouring families not partaking in the lavish parties the wealthy enjoyed, they could quite easily lose track of their age.

The same could happen with their place of birth. Perhaps the family had moved to Birmingham when the person was just a baby, so they always assumed they had been born there. Perhaps they couldn't remember where their parents had told them they had been born, so it was easier and more convenient to just say, 'Well I think I was born in (year) in (place).'

Sometimes lies were told when they married. Perhaps there was something they wanted to hide from their spouse, and not just the fact they were already married; a regular occurrence that is often shown by newspaper reports. A search of the Birmingham newspaper index for the second half of the 1800s shows about fifty reports of cases being brought to court, and that was just the ones that got found out. But there were other reasons for not giving the correct facts for the marriage certificate. Something they felt embarrassed about. They may have been pretending to be younger, or older. They may have been illegitimate and felt there was a stigma attached to it so gave a false name for their father, or sometimes gave their grandfather's name.

When someone died did the person registering the death really know how old the deceased person was? When asked this question a lot probably just said, 'I think he was around ...' So when searching for a birth on the basis of an age being taken from a death certificate and you can't find it in the year you thought it should be, search a few years either side.

While the internet is a good source for your research, you must always be aware that online databases can fall prey to human error. So anything found should always be checked on the original record. However, they are a very good pointer to take you to the correct entry in the original register, which also may give additional information that is not shown on the database. So this is another reason you should always check the original entry. Also, beware of any online family histories; again an interesting source but they can also give incorrect information. It is again down to human error and the assumption that the correct ancestor has been found. If it has not been followed up by the original researcher it can take you in the wrong direction. Again, never take these as fact, always follow up with your own research to decide if you are 100 per cent happy with what you are reading. On certain sites these family trees can be shared, which builds up a feeling of community but if one person has made a mistake then these mistakes are continued through to other family trees. Seeing an entry duplicated on numerous trees does not mean it is correct.

There are some good sites that use digital copies of original records and the subscriptions they charge compensate for any travelling expenses and the comfort of working in your own home. But at some stage you will need to visit the county record office and what a fascinating place a record office is. Have a good look around to see exactly what is there for the area you are interested in. Patiently search through the indexes and volumes to see if you can spot your ancestor's name or anything connected to your ancestor. Look to see what has been handed in for safekeeping. You'll be surprised what you might find. You might find a letter sent to or from a long-lost ancestor. You might even find a diary or perhaps a scrapbook of postcards and newspaper cuttings. The list of possibilities is endless. But, of course, it is only a possibility, not everyone is that lucky – but perhaps that one lucky researcher may be you!

For Birmingham these sorts of records are mainly kept in the Library of Birmingham and we shall talk about that later but first you have to make a start. Theoretically you have probably been given enough information to make a start with the 1939 register. So let's start here.

The 1939 Register

These records are only available on the internet at such sites as www.find-mypast.co.uk. There are many internet sites the family historian can use and we'll also talk about those later.

The register was taken on 29 September 1939 and was used to produce identity cards and ration books. You can search for a name or address or just browse by county and district. The information you find contained on the pages will give you the address, names, dates of birth, marital status and occupations for the people at that address. You will also see the other people along that street. For example, Arthur and Lily Coleman are living at 133 George Street. He is a timber carrier and general labourer who was born on 31 December 1914. Now it is highly unlikely that his birth was registered on the day of his birth so you would need to look at the first quarter of 1915. Sure enough, an Arthur Coleman was registered in Birmingham during the March quarter of 1915. The way the GRO indexes work will be explained later. However, unlike the census, the 1939 index doesn't give a place of birth, so you can only assume Arthur was born in Birmingham. But this is just an example of how you can progress your research from just one find. As you read on it will all fall into place.

You will see some blanked out lines across the pages. The details of anyone born less than 100 years ago, their death not having been proved, are intentionally blanked out and won't even appear on the index. So if using this index you really need to search for someone who you know has died. However, they are updating the pages every year and checking for deaths. You can also inform the site yourself if you know someone has died and they will check for the death then amend the record accordingly.

Even in the more modern days of the 1930s watch out for different ways of spelling names. The enumerator compiled the registers from the handwritten copies people filled in, so he may not have read someone's writing correctly. Another reason for not finding someone is that a very small number of people didn't register, as they thought it might prevent them from being conscripted. Of those few, some did get picked up by the officials and were made to give their details but some did go unnoticed.

You may see names that have been crossed out and changes made in different handwriting, in particular a woman who married after the register was taken. The register was constantly being updated as it was in use right through the war and then later for National Service purposes right up to

1952. It was also used by the National Health Service up until 1991. So if someone married or changed their name by deed poll their entry would be changed in the register. Certainly helpful to the family historian.

The Census

If you can't find someone in the 1939 register but you have enough details to take you back to 1911 you can start with the census. But, if you can't find who you're looking for in 1939 and, if you can't start with the census either, you'll have to use other methods first that will be talked about later. Incidentally, a census is only made available 100 years after it was taken so at the time of writing family historians are eagerly awaiting the arrival of the 1921 census, which will be released in January 2022.

So let's assume you have knowledge of an ancestor who was born in, say, 1910 and so can begin with the census of 1911. This census is different from the previous ones you will eventually search through. Here you see the form your ancestor filled in rather than the enumerator's schedule, together with additional questions that weren't asked on previous censuses. What you find on the 1911 form are all the names in the household, their relationship to the head of the household, their age, their marital status and how long they had been married, how many children they'd had and how many were still alive or had died. They were asked what their occupation was and where they worked together with their place of birth and their nationality. Perhaps the hardest question was if they had a disability. But this didn't just include deaf, dumb or blind, the words 'lunatic' and 'feeble-minded' were also added to the question. So by knowing how long a couple had been married you can start searching for their marriage. Give or take a couple of years for inaccuracy, which again we will talk about later.

Once you have found your family you now have the clues to take you back ten years to the 1901 census and then back every ten years to 1841. The clues are someone's age and place of birth, which can be used in a search engine, if using an internet site, or to confirm your ancestor against someone else with the same name in the vicinity if scrolling through a whole census.

The earliest census available, which is of use to the family historian, is the 1841 census. There were earlier 'head-counts', one as early as 1801, but the majority have not survived. Those that can be found only give the names of the residents, but of course are still interesting.

As mentioned before, with these pre-1911 census you are viewing a page from the enumerator's schedule that shows your ancestor's neighbours, too. These pages differ over the years. Your ancestor wasn't asked for the number of years they had been married or the number of children, dead or alive. You still see their occupation but not where they worked, just whether they were a worker or an employer. Between 1851 and 1881 you only see what their occupation was, although sometimes the enumerator has added the number of workers the person employed. That can give a clue to how affluent they were, for example at 7 Digbeth in 1871, John Keeling was listed as a 'fishing rod manufacturer employing 5 men and 2 youths'. Very often if your ancestor was a farmer the enumerator added the number of acres he farmed.

When we get back to 1841 this census is very different. All it shows is name, age and sex, occupation and if the person was born in that county. The age was usually rounded to the nearest five so you don't always get an accurate age. And with your ancestor only having to answer yes or no to the question 'were you born in this county', you just hope he lived until 1851 when he would state his exact place of birth, if you are researching forward for some reason, which at times you will find yourself doing.

Another pitfall with the 1841 census is the fact no relationships are shown. So don't assume when you see a list of names after the name of the head of the household that those are his children. They may be nieces or nephews who were staying with him at the time of the census. And two adults living together may not necessarily be husband and wife. They may be brother and sister.

Each household in the 1841 census is split by the symbol //, which helps when no specific address is given. And servants and non-family members in a household are split with a '/' from the family names.

Another pitfall with all censuses is finding your 12-year-old ancestor living with his parents. Don't assume the wife of his father is his mother. You may go back ten years when he is 2 and find his father has a different wife, who of course would be his mother. With many women dying in childbirth leaving their husband with a young family to look after it was very rare for a man not to remarry, often very quickly after the death of his wife.

Sometimes you may see a couple with a very young child and the mother's age seems a little too old, past her child-bearing years so-to-speak. Have a look at her older daughters – one of them might be the mother. Very often parents unofficially 'adopted' their daughters' illegitimate children to save any embarrassment. Also, take care with the way letters were written. It's very common for an L and an S to be written in a very similar way, so you may mistake your ancestor's occupation as lawyer thus giving him a much grander lifestyle than his actual occupation of sawyer.

Another anomaly is the relationship of son-in-law and daughter-in-law. You may see this description alongside a child of only 10. This means the child is a stepson or stepdaughter in our modern terms. The word 'step' wasn't introduced until the second half of the 1800s, and even then wasn't used a great deal, so it can be confusing.

Of course, all of the censuses give some kind of address but sometimes they are not that accurate, just giving the name of the village in a certain parish. But you can find the enumerator's journey at the start of each schedule so sometimes it is quite easy to follow him around as you scroll through the pages. For example, this piece taken from the 1881 census covering a district in the St Thomas' parish:

> The whole of the right hand side of Windmill Street from Windmill Hill to the Horse Fair. All the houses on Windmill Hill, the whole of Bow Street and Little Bow Street, part of the right hand of Bristol Street from the corner of Little Bow Street to Gt Colmore Street.

Also, be aware that the number that appears in the first left-hand column is not the house number but the number in the census schedule. Also, when a different house number is given for the same street in two different census it doesn't necessarily mean the family has moved house. Often house numbers changed if the street had further development.

An enumerator for the census was employed by the local registrar and paid a fixed sum. As an example, in 1871 an enumerator earned an initial one guinea but when they had visited 400 households they would receive an additional 2*s* 6*d* for each batch of 100 people they visited. They were also given 6*d* a mile for delivering the schedules and 6*d* a mile for collecting them. The job description of an enumerator was that they had to be intelligent and able to read and write to a reasonable standard – although when you see some of the pages from a census you might disagree with that. They had to be fit, bearing in mind they would have a lot of streets to walk around, aged between 18 and 65 and be respectable with temperate habits. It was also imperative that they knew the area well.

The enumerator would go around his district leaving a schedule with each householder prior to the census night then collect them the day after census night. He would query any entries on a schedule if necessary or if everyone in the household was illiterate, fill the form for them on the doorstep. Up until 1911 he then had to copy all the details into his enumerator's book and send it to the registry. From 1911 the enumerator's books ceased to be used as the registry accepted the householder's schedule.

Did our ancestors religiously fill the schedule in on the actual census night or did they just fill them in when it was convenient? It hasn't been unheard of for someone to be entered in two schedules depending on whether they just happened to be away from home on census night. Their family may have included them on their schedule because they lived at that house. But the person they were staying with took it more seriously and therefore included them on their schedule as they were staying there on census night. If they were in the same district, a keen enumerator may have been suspicious and double-checked with the households concerned but if two different districts were involved it would be very likely they would go unnoticed.

Our ancestors may have found the filling in of census forms difficult but it seems some enumerators found it just as hard, as this poem written anonymously in 1884 reveals. Called 'The Enumerators Complaint', it humourlessly confirms some of the problems also faced by those of today trying to trace their ancestors:

> The census may be good and right
> and useful to the human natur'
> But I can swear there's no delight
> In being an enumerator;
> For up and down six blessed streets,
> I've tramped it morning after morning,
> And the reception that one meets
> Should serve as a most wholesome morning
>
> This house, their writing isn't plain;
> That house, their language is exotic;
> And some describe themselves as sane,
> Who seem to me quite idiotic.
> Towns such as countless never knew
> Are given as the natal places;
> While you're supposed to find what's true,
> And to correct in faulty cases.
>
> Then ladies of a certain age
> Decline to make it clear by telling;
> And others fly into a rage,
> And oh, such awful slips and spelling!
> And some deduce – in humour bold –
> Their line from non-existent nations,
> And state they've grown uncommon old
> In most unheard of occupations.

Here, you perceive that you intrude;
And here, the party's an objector;
And here, they are positively rude –
They fancy you're the tax collector.
So what with humbug and rebuff,
And cutting many fruitless capers,
I have already had enough,
And cry – Confound these census papers!

Births, Marriages and Deaths

If you are not able to start your research in 1911 you will have to go to the General Register Office (GRO) indexes first. But you will soon incorporate these in your research anyway. The registration of births, marriages and deaths began in 1837 following two Acts of Parliament in 1836, the first being the Births and Deaths Registration Act and then the Marriage Registration Act. Following these acts the registration of births, marriages and deaths began in July 1837. The year was split into quarters: January, February and March, known as the March quarter; April, May and June, known as the June quarter; July, August and September, known as the September quarter; and October, November and December, known as the December quarter. The country was split up into registration districts with Birmingham and Aston being separate until 1912, when they amalgamated to become one district. Then, in 1924, the district was split into Birmingham North and Birmingham South before once again in 1932 becoming just the one district of Birmingham.

First you have to find the entry for your desired certificate in the separate indexes for births, marriages or deaths, which are listed in surname order. Again allow for any spelling discrepancies made by the registrar. For example, if you're looking for someone named Haynes, it could be spelt Haines, and if you still can't find it look under Ainge. Even a name such as Pearce can also be spelt Pierce, or Duffin as Daffin, Gateley as Gaitley and White as Whyte, to name but a few. In fact it is quite a good idea to take a name and list all the different ways you think it could be spelt, so you are always prepared.

An anomaly to mention here is that when searching the births indexes, if you don't find the birth you are looking for and have tried the years before and after the assumed date, always look at the end of the list for that surname. Sometimes if it was thought the child wouldn't survive the parents didn't give it a name so it was registered as either 'male' or 'female'.

So how do you know you have the correct name, particularly with a very common one. Marriages are easy. All entries on the GRO indexes show not only the district the event took place but also a unique reference number that consists of the volume number in which the event is entered and the page number in that volume. So search for both parties in the index, then check that the location and reference number agree for both names. If they do, you have the correct marriage. If they don't then you need to keep searching. For example, Charles Sturge married Elizabeth Summerfield in 1866. On the marriage index for Charles Sturge it can be found having been registered in Birmingham during the September quarter with a reference of 6d 17. If you then look at Elizabeth Summerfield, this also gives the district as Birmingham with a reference of 6d 17. However if you looked under Elizabeth Summerfield's name first you would see another Elizabeth Summerfield in that quarter having married in the King's Norton district with a reference of 6c 568. At first you might think that perhaps she had married in her neighbouring district of King's Norton but because you know her husband's name, checking his entry you immediately know which one was correct.

It gets a bit easier after 1916 as the spouse's maiden name is added to the index. Births and deaths can be a little more difficult, especially if it's a common name, but from 1916 you will get a small clue for a birth as after these years the birth indexes include the mother's maiden name on the index. From 1866 it can be reasonably easy with deaths as the age of the person was added to the indexes. However, if you use the General Register Office's own site (gro.gov.uk) to search for a birth or death you will find the mothers' maiden names listed from 1837 and the age of death also listed from 1837. However, at the time of writing the whole indexes haven't been added to the site yet.

Incidentally, having mentioned the names of Sturge and Summerfield it might be interesting to mention different name spellings again. The census shows Charles was born in Whichford in Warwickshire in 1838. But if you search for his birth in the Shipston on Stour district (the district to which Whichford belongs) you won't find it. Prior to Charles moving to Birmingham his name was spelt as Sturch and all his family are known as Sturch, so his birth is registered as Sturch. However, as soon as he is living in Birmingham his family name becomes Sturge. The same with Elizabeth Summerfield's ancestors, who came from Walsall in Staffordshire. If you were looking for them in the Walsall area you would find them as Sommerfield, and even as Sommerford in earlier registers.

So what information will you find on a certificate?

On a birth certificate, as well as finding who the parents were, you will find the mother's maiden name and this will assist in finding the parents' marriage. There will be the date the child was born. Very occasionally you may see a time given. When a time is included with the date it was because the mother had given birth to twins. The father's occupation and where the parents lived will be entered together with the date of registration and who registered the birth.

You may find the section for the father's name is left blank and realise the child was illegitimate. In theory this usually only happens after 1875 as it was after this time that, in order for the father's name to be included for an illegitimate child, he had to be present at the registration. Before then a mother could give whatever name she wanted, perhaps even making out she was married. But did this work? Presumably it would as the mother only had the one name to give the registrar – her maiden name rather than a married name and a maiden name. So wouldn't it be easy for her to lie and conceal the child was illegitimate? It all depends on how devious our ancestors were.

So although you probably want to follow all your branches back as far as you can, sometimes in this instance you have to be prepared to hit a brick wall (as genealogists say) with the father's line and continue with just the mother's.

A marriage certificate will tell you the fathers' names of both the parties and their occupations. Sometimes if a father had died the word 'deceased' may be added to his name or put as the occupation. Also entered is the date and where the marriage took place, be it a church, chapel or the register office itself, and the address the parties were living at the time of the marriage. But bear in mind this may only be the address they were staying at, at that time; it might not be their home address. Sometimes the ages of the couple are given, sometimes just the word 'of full age' or 'minor' are entered.

With a death certificate, one of the helpful entries is the person who registered the death. This might prove or disprove a relationship. The age will help ascertain a date of birth, taking into account any misinformation given by the person registering the death, and what your ancestor died from can lead to further investigation. Perhaps a coroner's inquest or newspaper report.

There may be times when you just can't find an entry in the GRO indexes. If you are looking for a birth prior to 1872 it could be that the parents never registered the child. Registration wasn't free so often parents who couldn't afford the fee just didn't bother and up until 1872 they could get away with it. But an Act of Parliament in 1872 made it law for births to be registered. In most cases the person present at the birth was expected to inform the registrar that a birth had taken place, then the parents had forty-two days to register the birth. But it's highly likely that a lot still slipped through the net.

With marriages, the person performing the ceremony had to inform the registrar, so if you can't find a marriage ask yourself: a) did they marry far from home, or b) did they marry at all? Even in those days it wasn't unheard of for a couple to not get married, and for the woman to just use the man's name rather than her own. But luckily it was quite rare.

A burial could only take place on receipt of a death certificate, so the only way a death could go missing was if the person died a long way from home. The problem then is that if it's a common name you might see it on the index but not realise it is yours.

As already mentioned, a marriage certificate might show a father as deceased, however, just because a father doesn't appear as deceased on his son's wedding certificate don't assume he was still alive. Remember, the official at the wedding who was entering the information only wrote down what he was told. When asked a father's name, the bride or groom might not have thought to say that he had died. And if one of them wasn't local, their family might not even attend the wedding and the official might not notice a missing father and ask where he was. So if you don't find a death after the marriage, look before it took place.

It is very simple to order a certificate online at the GRO's own website but if you're not sure you have the correct entry you can write direct to the Birmingham Registrar giving all the details you know, which they will check in their own indexes and if it is correct send you the certificate. Prices have changed over the years so it's best to check what the current fees are using their own webpage, birmingham.gov.uk/certificates.

Parish Registers

Eventually your research will take you to the parish registers and here, with luck, you can trace your roots right back to the sixteenth century. Of course, in a lot of cases you can bypass the 'obtaining certificates' part and go straight to using parish registers; the choice is yours. It's just that sometimes it's easier to find a marriage in the GRO indexes than searching through church records when you're not sure in which church the marriage may have taken place. And, of course, both birth and death certificates will give more details than a parish baptism or burial.

It was after the Act of Supremacy in 1534 and the formation of the Church of England that Thomas Cromwell decided registers should be kept for all baptisms, marriages and burials and on 5 September 1538 this became law. Anyone who didn't comply was given a fine of 3s 4d. The register was to be kept in a chest in the vestry and secured with two locks. Unfortunately for family historians, these early volumes were only made of paper and as they were kept in the damp conditions of old churches some have not survived.

It wasn't until 1598 that the law stated they should be made of parchment and at the same time all entries from the earlier registers, going back to the start of Elizabeth's reign, were to be copied into the new parchment volumes. For their age some are surprisingly easy to read but on the whole they can be very difficult and, of course, they can be obliterated by patches of damp or pieces having been ripped out. But to find something in one of these old registers is a family historian's dream. On the whole the Birmingham parish registers are very good and very clear, although some parts have been written in Latin, but the names and dates are still easy to read.

Between 1643 and 1660 there may be a gap in the register you are searching. During these years of the Commonwealth the keeping of registers was abolished, although some diligent clergy still maintained records. On the whole the parishes around Birmingham that were in existence at the time seem to have continued to keep registers. With a couple there seems to be a gap in the late 1640s and early 1650s but in most cases the events were still recorded.

Up until the eighteenth century baptisms, marriages and burials were recorded in whatever way the presiding vicar wanted them to be listed. Sometimes they are all written down together in date order. Or there may be separate pages for baptisms, separate pages for marriages and separate pages for burials. It was the same for the amount of information included. With baptisms it may be just a date, the child's name and the parents' names, although sometimes only the father's name was written down. There may also be additional information, such as the father's occupation and the place of abode. It is very rare though for the mother's maiden name to be included.

Marriage entries will, of course, tell you the names of the couple – that is the bride's maiden name – and the date of the marriage. Sometimes, if one of the parties was from a different parish this might be written down but on the whole it is just the two names.

With burials you usually just have a date and name. Sometimes, if it is a child, the father's name or parents' names are included, or a spouse's name if the person had been married. Occasionally an age, occupation or abode is given.

All registers were kept differently and the style also very often changed with a change of clergy.

On 25 March 1667 the Burying in Woollen Act was passed, which stated: 'No corpse of any person (except those who shall die of the plague) shall be buried in any shift, sheet, or shroud, or anything whatsoever made or mingled with flax, hemp silk, hair, gold, or silver, of any stuff, or thing, other than what is made of sheep's wool only.' A fine of £5 was levied on anyone who didn't adhere to the instructions.

The reason for this was that although there was an abundance of sheep in the country, the wool industry was in decline due to the amount of imported cloth coming in. So parliament decided to do something about it, particularly as many of their members had country estates that benefited from the sheep farmers. The Act was repealed in 1814 but had been mainly ignored for many years before then, the rich having felt they would rather pay the fine than not be buried in their best clothes.

The clergy were under instructions to keep records of those buried in wool, so certainly in the burial registers of the late 1600s and early 1700s you will see the words 'buried in wool' against a burial entry.

In 1754 the first Act to change the keeping of parish registers took place. The Hardwicke Marriage Act made it law that marriages should take place in an Anglican church, apart from those who were Jews or Quakers. All persons under the age of 21 had to provide parental consent, although the minimum age for marriage remained at aged 14 for a male and 12 for a girl. This age remained in place until 1929 when it was changed to aged 16 for both parties. So it is worth noting here that if you find a marriage and then go back in years to find a baptism, don't be put off if there is only a gap of twelve to fourteen years. In certain circles a marriage of convenience may take place, only to be annulled at a later date if circumstances changed.

This Act also changed the way marriage registers were kept. A new printed register was produced that gave clear instructions as to what information was to be given. Signatures, or a mark, were also required for both bride and groom and their witnesses. The standard format reads:

'......... (groom's name) of the parish of .... and .... (bride's name) of the parish of .... married in this church by .... (banns or license) this day of .... in the year One thousand Seven Hundred and .... by me .... (name of vicar). This marriage was solemnized between us .... (signatures or marks of couple) in the presence of .... (two witnesses signed or made their mark)

Sometimes the clerk would just write 'of this parish', but learning the place your ancestor was living is another step forward. If a different parish to where he is marrying, it is possible his family could be traced there. Or did he take his new bride home with him and that is where their children will be found?

Here it should be mentioned the difference between the description of 'by banns' and 'by licence'. The majority of marriages took place after the banns had been read on three consecutive Sundays. However, in some cases it was a desire to be married without the ceremony being advertised or without the three weeks wait or in a church other than their own parish church because they were marrying in secret. In these cases a couple would apply to the bishop for a licence, which also meant in theory they were asking the bishop for permission to marry and not their families.

The groom, together with his bondsman, who could be anyone of his choosing, would swear that there was no cause or impediment why he and his bride couldn't marry. He and his bondsman would then sign the Bond and Allegation to confirm they were telling the truth. If it was later discovered that lies had been told a fine would be issued. The

Bond and Allegation would be kept by the bishop and a licence would be given to the groom to present at the church chosen for the marriage. It was very rare for the licence to be kept with any parish registers but the Bond and Allegations were kept and are available to search the same as other parish papers.

So what will they tell you? They will give you a clue of where and when the marriage took place They will tell you the ages of the couple, whether they were single or widowed and the name of the bondsman may give a clue to someone else in the family, as obtaining a licence didn't always mean the family were excluded.

If for some reason you still can't find the marriage in the parish registers the Allegation does give the name of the groom's intended, so at least you now know your maternal three times great-grandmother's maiden name.

Some banns registers have also survived and are usually kept with the marriage registers. Although they don't give the exact date of the marriage, you will again find the bride's maiden name and also the parishes the couple lived in. The dates the banns were read will give you a clue of when the marriage took place and if the couple are from different parishes you will get a clue to search another set of registers.

The next Act to change the way parish registers were kept was the Rose's Act of 1812. From 1 January 1813 baptisms and burials were kept in separate printed registers. Pre-printed, the clergy had certain columns to fill in rather than just write a sentence.

For baptisms there was a column for the date, next was the Christian name or names of the child and then a column for the parents' Christian names. Their surname was in the next column, followed by their place of abode. There was another column for the father's occupation, then the name of the person who performed the baptism. But again it is very rare for the mother's maiden name to be entered.

For burials there were five columns: name, place of abode, date, age and the signature of the person who performed the burial.

The marriage registers changed in 1837 to comply with the format used by civil registration and since then all registers have remained exactly the same today.

Another act in 1836 gave Catholics and Nonconformists the right to marry in their own churches.

Bishop's Transcripts

The sending of transcripts of the parish registers to the bishop began in 1598, when the law required a second copy of registers be kept for the diocese. These sheets of parchment were sent to the bishop around Easter time and contained all baptisms, marriages and burials for the previous year. As far as family history is concerned, they are not as easy to search as the parish register, as you have to search by the year rather than the parish. First you have to go through the collections for a particular year looking for the parish you are interested in. Then, if you don't find the baptism, marriage or burial you are looking for you have to go to the next bundle for the next year and so on. So it can be a lot more time consuming. But if you can't find something in a parish register it is always a good idea to look in the Bishop's Transcript (BT) as the clergy were expected to be very diligent when recording for the bishop. Sometimes when filling in the details for the bishop they might suddenly come across a note of a baptism, marriage or burial they had forgot to enter in the register. It is very rare, but can happen so you may be lucky and find your elusive ancestor.

Birmingham belonged to the Diocese of Lichfield and Coventry so most of the BTs for the Birmingham district were kept at Lichfield Record Office. When it closed in 2018 the archives were transferred to Stafford Record Office. Parts of Birmingham that were once in the diocese of Worcester such as Northfield, King's Norton, Yardley are kept at the family history centre in The Hive in Worcester.

There is not a complete coverage for all the years the BTs were in existence and they were phased out with the introduction of civil registration, but can be useful nonetheless, and very often the writing is a lot neater, too.

Nonconformist Records

In this group we have Catholics, Baptists, Methodists, Presbyterians, Unitarians and many other smaller sects. So how do you find your nonconformist family? From 1841 they will appear on the census and from 1837 their events were recorded the same as anybody else's. But what about their parish registers? Unfortunately, without being too disheartening, this is where there may be a problem because, as the registers of nonconformists were kept by their officers and not in a church building, many have been lost along the way. Of those that have survived some have found their way into the Library of Birmingham.

Luckily, in 1837 the General Register Office collected many of the old registers, and those afterwards, and they are now kept in The National Archives (TNA) in Kew. But a good site, thegenealogist.co.uk, has joined forces with TNA to provide access to these registers.

Your Catholic ancestors are relatively easy to find as all their surviving records are kept in the archives at Cathedral House, St Chad's, Birmingham. There probably won't be any for earlier than the mid–1700s as the Catholics didn't keep records before that time for fear of detection. With various Acts of Parliament giving them rights they hadn't previously been allowed, such as having their own places of worship rather than meeting in secret in large houses, they began keeping their own methodical records. There is a searchable database of what is available on St Chad's website, www.birminghamarchdiocesanarchives.org.uk, but if you do find they hold the register you want to look through you will need to make an appointment to visit.

Using the Internet

White's *Directory* of 1849 tells us that, 'The town of Birmingham is now divided into five parishes, having fifteen churches besides six more with the borough in the parish of Aston.' The 1872 *Kelly's Directory* tells us that Birmingham and its suburbs had sixty churches and chapels. This figure increased rapidly, so you will find there is a lot to search through, especially as some, for example St Martin's, have numerous pages for baptisms that took place in just one day. But help is at hand. Ancestry.co.uk have now digitalised most of the registers for Birmingham and these can be searched by name. Clicking on the entry you think will be yours will take you straight to the page in the original register. You can also just browse through the digital pages the same as you would search the parish registers in the archives.

However, you must still take into account the errors in modern technology that come down to human error. Whoever compiled the index may have picked up the incorrect spelling of a name. Perhaps the entry wasn't clear, perhaps the spelling was different to today's way of spelling the name or perhaps there was some other distraction. So if you can't find your ancestor, don't give up. Remember, in most cases it will have been picked up exactly as it appeared in the register, so the person compiling the database will copy it as they see it. Try spelling the name a different way, even if it's not the way you know. Try putting just the surname in and the relevant year and see what comes up. As mentioned before, people were sometimes known by a different name throughout their life, sometimes using their middle name, so you might just spot your ancestor being baptised or married using their full name or the first name you didn't know they had. Perhaps try just entering the Christian name. You might spot a very unusual way the surname has been spelt.

There are other sites such as FindMyPast and TheGenealogist, which are also subscription sites. For free sites you have FamilySearch, which is organised by the Church of the Latter Day Saints and contains a database of the International Genealogical Index (IGI) which was compiled many years ago. This database contains parish baptisms and marriages of many parishes, but not all. It is very helpful in giving you a pointer to where you might find an event, but when found an entry must be checked just to make sure it is correct and to see if there is anything extra written down.

It is very difficult to mention all the genealogical sites available on the internet and it really is personal choice as to which you prefer. They all have many of the same records such as the 1939 register, the census and the GRO indexes but then they have other records only available to them. But you can search their indexes for what they offer before deciding to pay.

Another free and very useful site is the GRO's own website, gro.gov.uk/gro/content/certificates. Here you can order certificates online, either a hard copy or, in the case of certain years for a birth or death, a downloadable PDF copy. There is also the facility of searching for a birth or death. No doubt the facility for searching and ordering a PDF copy of a marriage, or other years for births and deaths, will soon be available. There are different prices for the different formats and also for how quickly the certificate will be sent to you.

There are many sites, some of which have been available for many years, that give all sorts of information and links to many resources. Just a web search will give you quite a list to search through but the popular ones include genuki.org.uk, cydislist.com and ukbmd.org.uk. One specifically for Birmingham and surrounding counties is midland-ancestors.uk, which is described as the public face of the Birmingham and Midland Society for Genealogy and Heraldry (bmsgh.org). Perhaps you may want to become a member; they have regular meetings all over the area. Or perhaps you can find another family history society nearer where you live (if you live away from your ancestors' place of birth). They are easy enough to find on the internet.

The Library of Birmingham

Although a lot of information can now be found on the internet, you will find the majority of registers, records and documents relating to your

Brummie ancestors are in the Library of Birmingham. There are two departments here, both of which operate very differently to each other.

The Heritage Research Area is open during normal library hours and holds the registers and records most commonly used by a family historian: microfilmed copies of parish registers, censuses, local newspapers and maps. All you need is a library ticket, which is easy to obtain on your first visit.

Adjoining this area, through a security gate, is the Wolfston Centre for Archival Research, where you can view the many collections kept by the library. The opening hours differ from the normal library opening hours and can be found on the libraries website. You also have to book an appointment in advance, either by telephone or email. To visit this area, as with most archives, you will need a County Archives Research Network (CARN) ticket. Again, you can easily get one on the day if you don't already have one. All you will need is some kind of proof of your address, a driving licence, bank statement or such-like.

It is easier and simpler if you can let the Wolfston Centre know the references of what you want to look at when you book. Perhaps on previous visits you may have looked through the card indexes and made a list of what you want to browse through on future visits. But if you haven't there are two places you can search to see what may be of interest.

The National Archives hold a catalogue for records held at record offices across the country that can be found at discovery.nationalarchives.gov.uk. It's better to use the advanced search tab, then scroll down to 'search other archives' and choose Birmingham Archives, Heritage and Photographic Service. Your search can be made up of any words you feel may apply to what you are looking for. You can use a specific name, or event or something specific such as 'poor law records', 'overseers', 'apprenticeship', etc., and a specific date range.

So, for example, if you search the word 'riots' you will find a list of archival bundles that contain papers concerning the Birmingham riots of 1791: letters, claims for damages, inventories of goods destroyed and more. One of the names mentioned in the descriptions of the various pieces of material is W.B. Bickley. If you do a search using his name you will see a list of other bundles that refer to his life and history such as deeds, letters and notebooks. Doing a search for a specific road, for example Hurst Street, will show the deeds and leases of the various people who lived or owned property there.

The other place to search is in the Library of Birmingham's own online catalogue at calmview.birmingham.gov.uk, where the principle of searching using any words is the same.

Some of your ancestors may have lived on the outskirts of Birmingham in parishes which in earlier times belonged to other counties. So it is always advisable to check the websites and use these record offices in your searches too, that is The Hive in Worcester and Warwick Record Office. Some may also have strayed into Staffordshire, so don't forget the Stafford Record Office.

The archives have a wealth of information and with so many records and documents having been given to them for safekeeping it's best to just take your time and browse and have fun finding that hidden gem.

3

Expanding your Roots

Or as a lot of family historians say, 'putting flesh on the bones'.

This research will now take you into the archives looking for anything that might tell you how your ancestors lived. It may be something personal to them or it may be something about where they lived or where they worked.

The list for this type of research is endless. There is what is known as the parish chest, registers that were used in the running of the church. Then there are the Poor Law records. There are newspapers, court records, cemeteries, wills and inventories. The list sometimes seems never ending.

The Parish Chest

First let's look at the parish chest and what that holds. From 1601 until 1834 everyone's life was practically ruled by their parish. Officials were elected each year from the more affluent men of the parish and they would take the roles of the churchwardens and the Overseers of the Poor. The churchwardens were the more senior of parish officials. They took charge of the running of the church and were responsible for its upkeep, its possessions and its grounds.

The Overseers of the Poor were there for those who needed financial help. But more often than handing out money they preferred to give assistance in the form of clothing or food. That way the poor were discouraged from using their benefits for the purchase of drink. They also found work for those who were fit enough to work and arranged apprenticeships for the children of the poor or any who had been orphaned. They also collected the poor rate.

The poor rate was a tax levied on the more wealthy parishioners; those who owned or leased property and land and those with a prosperous trade. The amount they paid, which was collected annually, was based on the value of their property. So finding any Poor Rate Books and finding your ancestor in one of these will show you how wealthy he was and if he prospered as the years went by.

Unfortunately though, not all the registers and papers belonging to the parish have survived but if you find some, even if your ancestor never had to go cap-in-hand to the parish, they can certainly give you an idea of what life was like.

So what can be found in the parish chest. Firstly there are …

Vestry Meeting Minutes

Vestry meetings were held regularly by the parish officials and those needing assistance, or relief as it was known, would present themselves at the vestry with their request. It was often just a one-off request for perhaps a new pair of shoes or a new coat. Sometimes they may be asking for assistance towards their rent while they were unemployed. The minutes would be taken for every request that came before the overseers, so looking through these will show you if your ancestor needed help. If their name didn't appear … well, hopefully, that means their life was trouble-free financially.

The minutes show the amount the person asked for and whether it was 'allowed' or 'not allowed'. Sometimes our poor ancestor was given something towards his request – 'allowed one pound towards it'. Or perhaps the request was for a new pair of shoes and a new coat. Our ancestors would be lucky if they got both. Very often the shoes would just be mended and a new coat given. Perhaps the shoes were mended but our ancestor was told to also repair his old coat.

It is quite often the case that the same people appeared on a regular basis. Sometimes you will see they are given so much per week towards their rent, then a few weeks later a decision might be made to reduce those payments, or perhaps stopped altogether because our ancestor had found work.

Settlements and Removals

The poor were considered to put a burden on the parish, so the overseers were very careful about who they assisted. They only wanted to help people who were 'settled' in the parish. They didn't want people just coming in, falling into dire straits, then expecting to be given help. So very often, if someone was asking for help, they would have to undergo a settlement examination that, if they passed, entitled them to a settlement certificate. If any can be found, they are useful in finding where your ancestor was born if he wasn't alive when the census was taken and a baptism cannot be found in the parish in which he married or was buried.

Legal settlement was granted if a person:

Rented property at £10 per annum
Had worked in the parish for a year
Was the wife of a man from the parish
Was the legitimate child, aged 7 or under, whose father lived in the parish
Was an illegitimate child born in the parish
Was an apprentice hired by a parishioner
Paid parish rate or was a parish official
Had lived in the parish for forty days and had given written notice of this intention.

So here is an example of someone who, according to the census was born in Birmingham, but whose father proves to be elusive. Finding the settlement examination of his father tells you exactly what happened. William Parsonage was born in Birmingham on 10 March 1827, the son of William and Sarah Parsonage, and was baptised at St Philip's on 10 July 1829. The entry tells you that his father William was a gardener, but you know nothing else about him. From other research your suspicions lead you outside Birmingham to a small parish in Worcestershire called Feckenham, where some settlement examinations have survived. Here you find one for William Parsonage Snr, which tells you that he was born in Northfield but moved to King's Norton with his family when he was just a boy. After working for various people on an annual basis, during which time he married his wife Sarah, he moved to Birmingham, where his son William was born. After four years he moved his family to Feckenham. You now know where to start searching in order to go further back, knowing William Snr was born in Northfield.

If the examination was not acceptable, a decision would then be made as to which parish was responsible for the person or family. When the decision was made, a removal order would be issued to have them returned to that parish. They would be taken by a parish constable to the parish boundary, where they were met by another constable of the neighbouring parish who would in turn take them to the boundary of his parish, if more than one parish had to be crossed.

In some cases a complaint could be made about a person, or a whole family, to the Justices of the Peace. They would take the case up and the offending party would appear at the quarter sessions (more on these later) and this was then usually followed by the issuing of a removal order.

A typical removal order would read:

To the Churchwardens and Overseers of the Poor of the Parish of .... in the County of .... and to the Churchwardens and Overseers of the Poor of the Parish of .... – Upon the complaint of the Church wardens and Overseers of the Poor of the Parish of .... aforesaid, in the said County of .... unto us whose Names are hereunto set and Seals affixed, being two of his/her Majesty's Justices of the Peace in and for the said County of .... and one of us of the Quorum, that ....

has come to inhabit in the said Parish of ...., not having gained a legal Settlement there, and is actually become chargeable to the said Parish of .... We the said Justices, upon due Proof made thereof, as well as upon the Examination of the said .... upon oath as otherwise, and likewise upon due consideration had of the Premises, do adjudge the same to be true; and we do likewise adjudge, that the lawful Settlement of him the said .... is in the said Parish of .... in the said County of .... We do therefore require you the Churchwardens and Overseers of the Poor of the said Parish of .... or some or one of you, to convey the said .... from and out of your said Parish of .... to the said Parish of .... and him deliver to the Churchwardens and Overseers of the Poor there, or to some or one of them, together with this our Order, or a true Copy thereof. And we do also hereby require you the said Church-wardens and Overseers of the Poor of the said Parish of .... to receive and provide for him as an inhabitant of your said Parish. Given under our Hands and Seals, the ...... day of .... in the year of our Lord One ...

Apprenticeship Indentures

If families fell on hard times and had a number of children, the overseers would often decide that some of those children should be sent out to work as apprentices and very often children as young as 7 would be sent to masters sometimes miles away from their families. This was considered advantageous to their own parish as it meant they would then become chargeable to that parish and not be sent back if they required relief later in life. The overseers would make the harsh decision at the Vestry Meeting, then find a suitable employer, who they would pay for the privilege of having free labour. A typical Apprenticeship Indenture would read:

This indenture, made the ...... day of .... in the .... year of the Reign of our Sovereign Lord .... by the Grace of God, of Great Britain and Ireland, King, Defender of the Faith, and so forth; and in the

year of our Lord One Thousand .... Witness that ....
Church-Wardens of the Parish of .... in the County of .... And
.... Overseers of the Poor of the said parish, by and with consent
of his/her Majesty's Justices of the Peace for the said County have put and
placed, and by these presents do put and place .... A poor Child of
the said Parish, Apprentice to .... With him/her to dwell and
serve from the day of the date of these presents, until the said Apprentice
shall accomplish his/her full Age of Twenty one years [sometimes the
words until the day of marriage were added] according to the Statute in
that case made and provided. During all which term the said Apprentice
his/her said Master/Mistress faithfull shall serve in all lawful business,
according to his/her Power, Wit and Ability, and honestly, orderly, and
obediently, in all things demean and behave him/her self towards his/her
said Master during the said Term. And the said .... For him/her self,
his/her Executors, and Administrators, doth Covenant and Grant, to and
with the said Church-Wardens and Overseers, and every of them, their
and every of their Executors and Administrators, and their and every of
their Successors, for the time being, by their presents, that the said ....
the said Apprentice in the art of .... shall teach or cause to be taught
and instructed in the best manner he can; And shall and will during all of
the term aforesaid, find, provide, and allow, unto the said Apprentice, meet,
competent, and sufficient Meat, Drink, and Apparel, Lodging, Washing,
and all other Things, necessary and fit for an Apprentice. And also shall
and will to provide for the said Apprentice, that he be not any way a
Charge to the said Parish, or Parishioners of the same; but of and from all
Charge shall and will save the said Parish and Parishioners harmless and
indemnified during the said Term. In witness whereof, the Parties above
said to these present Indentures, interchangeably have put their Hands and
Seals, by the Day and Year above-written.

Unfortunately many masters did treat these children as free labour, not
giving them the training they had agreed, not feeding them adequately, and
giving them horrendous places to sleep. This led to many children eventually

running away. Having lost their cheap labour, the masters would not hesitate in giving notice of a runaway in the newspaper, as the following shows:

> Went away from his master Mr Richard Lakin, shoemaker in Moor Street, on Saturday the 24th August 1743; John Brown about 19 years of age, lame on his right side, fresh coloured with straight hair, had on when he went away a brown cape coat, with yellow buttons and has just one year to serve. This is to forewarn all persons from employing him and to desire any who may know where he is to inform the said master and they shall receive all reasonable charges.

If no apprenticeship indentures have survived you may still find your ancestor was sent away as an apprentice and to who. A note would have been made in the vestry meeting minutes and the amount paid to the master would be entered in the accounts.

These types of apprenticeships should not be confused with those whereby an older child and his family chose to become an apprentice in order to learn a trade. In these cases the family would search for an appropriate master of whom they approved and enter into an agreement. Indentures of these kind occasionally find their way into the archives by having been included in a bundle of personal family papers or business documents.

Bastardy Bonds

If a woman fell pregnant with an illegitimate child it was highly likely she may need relief from the parish if the man didn't want to or couldn't marry her and she had no family to support her. In a lot of cases the overseers would be keen to find out who the father was so the woman would be asked to take an oath before the Justices of the Peace giving his identity. An example of the oath would be:

The examination of .... of .... in the county of .... single woman taken upon her Voluntary Oath before .... of his/her Majesty's Justices of the Peace in and for the said County this ...... day of .... one thousand .... touching her pregnancy. This Examinant saith That she is now with child or children and that .... of .... had carnal Knowledge of Her Body on or near the .... last past, whereby he did begat her with child, of the child or children wherewith she is now Pregnant, which is or are likely to be born in Bastardy, and to be chargeable to the parish of .... And this Examinant further saith on her Oath that the said .... Is the true and real Father of the said child or children

The father would then receive a visit from the overseers, who would try to persuade him to marry the woman. If he didn't he would be issued with a Bastardy Bond agreeing to give financial assistance for the child when it was born.

These were only in existence before 1834 and unfortunately not many have survived but you may be lucky and find one for your illegitimate ancestors of which, surprisingly, you will probably have quite a few.

Overseers' Accounts

These show what was paid out following a vestry meeting, so if no vestry meetings exist and if you find a bundle of overseer's accounts, you may still discover your ancestor had fallen on hard times. Of course, if your ancestor's request was refused at the vestry meeting you won't find him here in the accounts. They are not as explicit as the vestry meetings and won't show you how much or what your ancestor had actually asked for but will show you what he received and why.

Churchwardens' Accounts

The churchwardens' accounts show the financial side of running the parish and the church, and include payments out and payments in. Payments in usually relate to rentals of property owned by the church or money bequeathed in a will. Payments out can be for all sorts of things, some one-off payments, some regular. Regular payments could be the fee paid to the church organist. So if your ancestor was the organist for a church you will see how much he earned. Or a one-off payment could be to someone who repaired the pathway to the church.

Parish officials would claim their expenses through the churchwardens' accounts, such as taking someone who was being removed to the borders of the parish. So once again perhaps your ancestor may be named as someone being sent back to their parish of settlement. If no removal certificates have survived for this parish and the church warden's accounts have then you will have an answer for what happened to members if your family.

And so to end on a general note with regards to what might be available in the parish chest. It is always worth searching all these books and papers where available for your desired parish as something of interest may be there.

The Workhouse and the Poor Law Unions

The Poor Law Amendment Act of 1834 abolished the work undertaken by the parish overseers and the poor became the responsibility of Poor Law Unions. These unions were run by a board of governors and the parishes were grouped together into one local union. The Birmingham district was split into three unions, with the central parishes being taken care of by the Birmingham Union. The parishes within Sutton Coldfield, Castle Bromwich, Erdington and Aston fell into the Aston Union and the King's Norton Union covered the parishes of Selly Oak, Northfield, Harborne,

Edgbaston and King's Norton. In a later chapter 'Life in Birmingham' more will be told of the history of the workhouses.

Unfortunately, although the guardians were very good at keeping records, not many have survived. What has survived is held in the archives of the Library of Birmingham and can be found by searching the catalogue. You may find a few admission registers but not for all years. There are also the minutes of meetings held by the guardians. Searching these minutes, you may find a mention of one of your ancestors but even if you don't they will give you an idea of what everyday life was like in the workhouse. You can also search the census, which will show you if one of your ancestors lived in the workhouse at the time, although sometimes the enumerator was only given initials and not the full name, which is a bit frustrating for family historians.

You may find your ancestor's birth certificate gives the place of birth as 1 Western Road. This means they were born in the workhouse as that is its address in Birmingham. In this instance the officials were being kind and instead of using the words 'workhouse', which may be embarrassing for the child later in life, they used the address.

There were regular reports in the newspaper following any meetings of the board of guardians, so it is always worth searching for these. You probably won't find your pauper ancestor mentioned by name and sometimes there is nothing of real interest for the family historian, but you will get an idea of how the workhouse was organised. There were reports regarding the appointments of the guardians, medical officers, masters and matrons (perhaps your ancestor was named among these) and the financial accounts. Letters of complaints that had been made about the workhouse were also read out, such as a former inmate complaining of being mistreated or given a punishment they didn't deserve. Tenders were read out together with the names of the traders wanting to supply the workhouse, and the successful candidate reported. Again, perhaps your ancestor will be listed here.

Not all the traders were honest though as in May 1856 it was reported that there had been a complaint regarding the flour not being made to the correct standard as rice and maize had been added. The bread had too much water in it, so went mouldy quickly, and the milk was also watered down.

In July 1865 the newspaper reported of a cholera outbreak:

A report was read from Mr Robinson, the medical officer, in which he stated that 263 cases had occurred almost simultaneously about midnight on the previous Friday. The attack consisted of diarrhea, with nausea, blueness of the lips, cramp, and coldness of the extremities. Every case was promptly treated, and no deaths had occurred.

Newspapers

Newspapers appeared in Birmingham as early as 1732, when the *Birmingham Journal* was first published, and was closely followed by *Aris's Birmingham Gazette* in 1741. Reading old newspapers can be a mine of information but obviously they can be very time consuming to search if you haven't got a specific date to look at. However, there are two very good sites that take you straight to a digitised copy of the newspaper you need.

The British Newspaper Library has set up a website for all their newspapers and although not complete yet it is being added to all the time. The site www.britishnewspaperarchive.co.uk is a subscription site but if you already subscribe to FindMyPast there is a link to the newspaper archive here. All you have to do is enter your ancestor's name in the search, or any other keyword, and all related articles will be listed. Then, clicking on a relevant title will bring up the digital image of the original page. If you're not sure when someone died, search their name to see if there is an obituary or death notice.

Sometimes it's just as interesting to browse a newspaper published during an ancestor's lifetime. You'll find out what was happening in those times, what your ancestors may have been interested in and what people your ancestors may have known were doing. They are local history books written at the time. You may think that with most of our ancestors being illiterate, why would they be interested in newspapers? Although this is true, they still had an opportunity to hear what the newspapers were saying. Often a local person would organise a reading session somewhere, very often the local inn, where newspapers were read to groups interested in what was happening.

There are adverts that will make you wonder what on earth your ancestor may have been buying such as:

Oriental Vegetable Cordial 'for disorders of the stomach and bowels'.
Christian's Dandelion Chocolate 'invaluable to persons who may be predisposed to afflictions of the liver, spasms, flatuency, weak digestion or general debility'.
Macassar Oil 'rendering the human hair soft, glossy and consequently beautiful'.
Union Hairbrush 'the newly invented hair brush which entirely supersedes the use of the small tooth comb, promotes agreeable and salutary sensations to the head'.

There are jobs advertised, houses for sale or rent. All of these will help you build up a picture of what life was like for our ancestors at a particular time.

Searching a newspaper can lead to research in other records. For example you may find a death led to a coroner's inquest. Or an ancestor may have committed a crime. If you had wealthy, influential ancestors their wedding may have been reported in the newspaper. Certainly notices were announced of forthcoming marriages but for a notable person a report would follow describing the bride's outfit, who the bridesmaids were, what they were wearing and the gifts the couple received.

Perhaps you would like to know what your richer ancestors may have been wearing. There are regular reports of social events where the clothes worn by those attending are described in detail. With no illustrations like we have today in magazines, the descriptions can be very graphic, as this from 4 January 1851 shows:

Magnificent stamped material of sky blue with embroidered bouquets in white and silver, the bottom of the front breadth was embroidered (in the form of an apron) with large flowers, fastened with light hanging foliage and large bows, the skirt was raised over a white satin under-skirt by two bouquets composed of leaves of blue velvet and some small feathers mixed with silver cords; the same kind of bouquets were plaited in the hair, over which was worn a very light silver net-work. The body of this pompadour robe was trimmed with a new and beautiful fringe of white and blue feathers which harmonises well with the white shoulders it encircles.

You can read letters your ancestor may have written to the newspaper, such as this one written by Edwin Yates, the Mayor of Birmingham, and published in the *Birmingham Journal* on 10 March 1866:

Sir – Will you kindly caution the public against an imposition now being practised?

A person described as a genteel young man, and representing himself as a relative of mine, is calling upon gentlemen and stating that it is my wish he should solicit subscriptions towards a fund that is being raised for the purpose of procuring a life governorship of the Hospital for Idiots at Red Hill, and that myself and friends are interesting ourselves to obtain the entry of a boy into the institution.

The first part of the representation ought to have convinced those who have been imposed upon that it was an attempt to defraud, and after the numerous exposures in the public press of such cases, it is somewhat extraordinary that gentlemen continue to part with their money without making due enquiry.

So here we have a case that shows you cold-calling and obtaining money by deception happened to our ancestors, too.

You may come across a letter that shows you what the young boys in your family may have been getting up to, like this one which was published in *Aris's Birmingham Gazette* on 26 October 1857 and written by someone signing himself as simply 'Corns':

> Sir – I really must give up travelling by the North-western railway, unless the Directors will give me a private entrance from Queen Street, for the Stephenson Place approach is so infested by shoe-black boys that a nervous man can scarcely venture down it. I have been repeatedly assailed by these enterprising young gentlemen, one after the other; and, I confess it, have been made angry by their vociferous entreaties to permit them to 'black' my boots, that I have been tempted to conflict upon each of them a little useful 'polishing'. Sir, I tried to silence my persecutors by threats, by assumed indifference, and by politely declining their repeated proffers, but I failed in every attempt. At last I tried a little quiet argument. No sooner had I emerged from the station gates than an intrusive young urchin suddenly quitted his game of pitch-and-toss and ran towards me yelling out 'Black yer boots Sir?' I explained to him that my boots had very recently been 'blacked' at home, that I was not in the habit of submitting to that operation in the streets and with all the confidence of an injured logician I put it to him – 'Now do my boots want blacking?' The rascal looked at the boots, then at me, then winked at his companion and replied, amidst a shout of laughter, 'Yes sir they does; they'm very dirty.' Ever since that fatal encounter I have dreaded to enter Stephenson Place for my appearance is always the signal for a series of cries of – black your boots sir?

You may find someone who you thought an ordinary ancestor but who was well known and well loved by the people of Birmingham, as this report in the *Birmingham Mail* on 15 May 1931 shows:

> Birmingham's Oldest and Best Known Flower Seller – With brief formality the passing of one of Birmingham's most familiar figures was entered today on the records of the Coroner's Court with a verdict of accidental death. Known as Grandma Bibb to companion flower sellers and some of her customers in the centre of the city, for many years, in all

weathers, her station had been by the pavement's edge in Corporation Street, near Fore Street.

Of course, if your ancestor was a criminal their court appearance would be reported in the newspaper. These reports will actually give you more details than the court record does.

Another good newspaper is the *London Gazette*, which can be found at www. london-gazette.co.uk. First published in 1665, contained in its pages you will find all sorts of public notices – official appointments and army commissions, royal and government proclamations, details of wills and bankruptcies, insolvency notices and notices of business partnership dissolutions. Of course, you may have a specific name to search for but making a search with the word 'Birmingham' brings up tens of thousands of results. These results, or your search, can be filtered down by selecting a year or period of years. It is free to search but you will need to register in order to use the site,

Court Records

Birmingham seems to be one of the few places where its coroner's reports are still available. These are held at the Library of Birmingham and cover the years from 1875. There is a seventy-five-year closure restriction but you can request a copy of more recent inquests by writing to the coroner's court at 50 Newton Street.

The copies in Birmingham Archives can vary in size from a few sheets to huge bundles. They include the letter from the doctor, hospital or police informing the coroner of the death and the notice of when and where the inquest will be taking place. The size of the investigation will then be reflected in the number of pages that follow. There may be only one or two witnesses to be interviewed, there may be several. In the case of a road accident there may be maps of the area. Very often the clerk will write all the statements in an abbreviated form, but it is easy to follow; the problem occurs when they decided to put everything down in shorthand, and if you don't know shorthand it can be very soul-destroying knowing there is so much information there that you just can't access.

This is an example of a short inquest that took place at the Victoria Courts on Wednesday, 30 November 1898 at 2.30 p.m.

James Young, physician and surgeon, of 55 Digbeth, had informed the coroner of the sudden death of George Bedford stating that, 'Deceased had been a very heavy drinker but up to yesterday seemed in his usual health. Yesterday as his wife says he said he must be ill as he could not drink his beer. He went to bed as usual and got out of bed about 3 am, and in attempting to get into bed again fell dead across it. No marks of violence.'

George's widow, Fanny Bedford, appeared at the inquest and said that:

He has been a heavy drinker for many years. Frequently intoxicated, worse the last three weeks. Has complained of pains over his heart at times the last few weeks. He often thought he would faint and fall in the street. Had a fit seven years ago and was attended by Dr Kenny of Weaman Row and he said it was due to drink. He was the worse for drink on Saturday night. Went out at 1 pm. Sunday, returned 2.30 pm., and said, 'I must be ill. I have to refuse my beer.' He went to bed – got up 5 pm. Complained of cold – shivered – thirsty. I gave him soda and milk. Went to bed at 9 pm., – no supper. At 2.30 am., Monday got out of bed and used chamber. Got up and fell across the bed unconscious. I got him into bed and he died directly. I called a lodger named Jim from the attic. I then fetched Dr Young of Digbeth.

A further paper tells us that, 'The lodger James Mack confirmed that George was deceased when he was called from the attic.' And a final sheet states, 'Cause of death – natural causes – heart failure.'

Turning now to criminal courts, the assizes dealt with the most severe crimes such as murder or grievous assault, robbery and forgery and the more serious civil matters. They were presided over by a judge visiting from Westminster and originally took place twice a year in Lent and summer

South Yardley Cemetery showing one of its impressive entrances typical of Victorian cemeteries. (Author's Photograph)

until the mid-nineteenth century. From that period a third court was added during the winter.

The country was divided into six circuits: Home, Midland, Norfolk, Northern, Oxford and Western. The judges would travel around a circuit visiting the towns in each county that had a court room and hold their courts.

Up until 1884 Birmingham had no court of its own so all cases were heard in the Warwick court, which belonged to the Midland Circuit. So your ancestor who was involved in a case, be it as the accused or as a witness, had to travel to Warwick to attend the court. The first assizes in Birmingham were heard in August 1884 in the banqueting hall of the Council House, prior to the building of the Victoria Law Courts.

For ancestors living on the outskirts that belonged to other counties, you will find they may well have travelled to another court. For example,

The atmosphere of searching for grave stones in old cemeteries. This is just one small section of the large South Yardley Cemetery. (Author's Photograph)

with King's Norton belonging to Worcestershire, which was in the Oxford circuit, their cases were heard in Worcester.

In 1972 the assizes were replaced by the crown court.

Unfortunately not a lot of records for the assizes have survived. Old records were destroyed when the assizes' clerk ran out of space, but what has survived is kept at The National Archives in Kew. However, they were widely reported so you can read all about the case in the newspaper. Sometimes just one case could take up a whole page, sometimes just one paragraph. Obviously it depended on the severity of the case.

If you want to find if your ancestor did ever appear at the assizes, a small bundle of the Calendar of Prisoners is available on Ancestry.co.uk under the title of 'England & Wales, Criminal Registers, 1791–1892'. Searching a name will bring up the digital pages, which tell you the date and place of the court, name of the prisoner, their offence, previous convictions and whether convicted or acquitted and the sentence they received.

FindMyPast also has access to criminal records under its link, 'Crime, Prisons and Punishment 1770–1935'. As has been said before, these sites, and others, are adding more digital records on a regular basis.

The quarter sessions were held in the Public Office in Moor Street by the Justices of the Peace, who met at Epiphany, Easter, Midsummer and Michaelmas and covered what were considered less serious criminal matters such as theft, poaching, trespassing, vagrancy and minor assaults. They also dealt with certain parish matters such as removals and bastardy examinations, and other civil matters such as tax, licensing of public houses or trades. They considered if a person had been treated unfairly, they decided on the amount of payments that should be made by the father of an illegitimate child and approved the placing of pauper children as apprentices. They also examined the books and accounts belonging to the parish officers to make sure everything was correct.

The Justices of the Peace, also known as magistrates, were made up of the wealthy men of the town, landowners and business men. Quite often they had had no real legal training but they were wealthy enough to be discouraged from taking bribes. They could issue fines and prison sentences but were unable to impose harsh sentences such as death or transportation.

In 1972 the quarter sessions were amalgamated with the assizes to become the crown court. There are records for the quarter sessions in the Library of Birmingham under reference QS/B but again you will also find reports in the newspapers.

The petty sessions covered the less serious of both criminal and civil matters and were generally held once a week in the public office, but occasionally every day. Again they were reported regularly by the newspapers but records are available in the library under reference PS/B. They are now known as the magistrates' courts.

Cemeteries

By the early-mid nineteenth century the large expanding towns of England were discovering their churchyards were no longer large enough to offer final resting places for our ancestors, and Birmingham was no exception. The first cemetery in Birmingham opened in 1836.

Key Hill (Kayes Hill) Cemetery, named after a family who lived there centuries before, was built on former sandpits on Icknield Street by the Birmingham General Cemetery Company as a place for nonconformists to be buried. Twelve years later Warstone Lane Cemetery, also on disused sandpits, was opened by the Birmingham Church of England Cemetery Company to ease the burden of the burial grounds in the parish churches. Other cemeteries followed. Witton Cemetery, the largest of the three, was built in 1863 on Moor Lane and became the Birmingham City Cemetery. Sutton Coldfield Cemetery was opened in 1881, South Yardley Cemetery in 1883, Lodge Hill Cemetery, Selly Oak in 1895, Brandwood End, Kings Heath in 1899 and Handsworth Cemetery in 1909.

The registers for these cemeteries are kept in the Library of Birmingham. However, they are not quite as specific as church burial registers. You will only find the year your ancestor was buried and the reference number and grave number. With this information you can contact the relevant office for the cemetery to request further details and a map of where the grave is situated. There is a charge made for this service.

However, there are online indexes you can search. Birmingham Council have set up a site, birminghamburialrecords.co.uk, on which you can search by name and then purchase online digital copies of the burial record. At the time of writing the charge is £20. The registers differ from cemetery to cemetery, year to year, but the information you may get is the name, age, occupation and marital status of the deceased, the last place of residence and/or place of death and the date of death and burial. In some cases there will be a description of the grave, which will tell you who purchased the plot, unless it was a public grave, and who else was buried in this grave.

Public graves were very common in the nineteenth century as the poorer people couldn't afford to buy a cemetery plot. They were large plots that could contain as many as eight coffins and are now displayed as large areas of grass with no markers or monuments. However, just occasionally a stone may have been erected many years later by relatives of the deceased who had prospered.

On FindMyPast you will find the National Burial Index (NBI). This is a volunteer project commenced many years ago by family history societies all over the country. Coverage hasn't been completed yet but there is quite a good record for Birmingham.

Monumental inscriptions can be very elaborate with whole poems written, whereas others just give names and dates. During the 1950s and '60s the Society of Genealogists began a survey of numerous burial grounds all over the country and wrote down as many monument inscriptions as they could. These volumes can be found in the Library of Birmingham and can be useful if your ancestors could afford a stone marker for their grave. In more recent times the data was copied on to CDs to be used on home computers but now, certainly for Birmingham monuments, they are available to download from midland-ancestors.shop.

Of course, there is nothing more satisfying than visiting the grave yourself, even if it is only a public grave with no inscription to read. Take a camera with you just in case there is an elaborate monument to photograph. Unfortunately the passing of time, together with the loss of the descendants who originally looked after them, has not been kind to these personal memorials. Many are obliterated with moss, ivy and corrosion. However, armed with a map of the cemetery and knowing the grave number should take you to the correct grave.

Wills and Probates

If your ancestor left a will, sometimes it not only gives you the names of a spouse, children or other family members, it can also give you an insight into that person's thoughts; what they felt about the person who they wanted to remember in their will. Perhaps he or she was a faithful servant who served them for many years, or it had been a friendship that had lasted a lifetime. They will, of course, also show you how wealthy an ancestor was.

Some wills may be just short passages naming just one person; some may be many pages long naming numerous people with a long list of personal possessions or properties. Very often you will only find wills for a male ancestor. Husbands often left provisions in their wills for their wife that made it unnecessary for her to make her own will.

Before 1782 it was a legal requirement for an inventory to be taken of the deceased's property and these are usually attached to the will. One of these will really give you an insight into how your ancestor lived as everything he owned was accounted for – his wearing apparel and money, each room in his house would be listed and details of all the furniture in that room, what implements and equipment he used for his work, what livestock he had; everything was there.

Before 1858 the majority of wills were proved by the diocese, so the office copies are kept at the relevant record office. Most pre-1858 Birmingham wills were lodged at Lichfield Record Office, but since its closure have now been moved to Stafford Record Office. But once again FindMyPast comes to the rescue as they have digitised the indexes, so if you find an entry for a will you can contact Stafford Record Office to purchase a copy, if you are unable to go yourself. Some wills would have been proved in Worcester, so therefore will be held at The Hive in Worcester. But, again, there is an online index on FindMyPast.

Other wills were proved in the Prerogative Court of Canterbury. The main reason for this was if property was owned in two different dioceses. For this court there is an index on the TNA website discovery. nationalarchives.gov.uk. From there you can download, for a small charge, a copy of the will.

From 1858 the Principal Probate Registry was introduced and the country split into various districts. Birmingham had its own district and the indexes and fully transcribed wills for Birmingham from 1858–1941 are kept in the Library of Birmingham. However, there is an official online index that covers all years from 1858 up to the present day that can be searched at www.gov.uk. Follow the link 'births, deaths, marriages and care', then 'Search probate records'. Once you have found the deceased's name in the index you can click to purchase a digital copy. The present cost is £1.50. Alternatively, hard copies can be purchased from the relevant probate registry at a cost of, currently, £6.

Directories

Trade and Post Office directories can give you an insight into your ancestor's business or trade as you follow him through the years from when he started until when he ended. But directories also list residential properties, so are useful to find someone in between the census years. However, unlike the census, they don't list everybody, only those who chose to pay an annual fee in order to appear in a directory.

The Library of Birmingham has numerous shelves of directories published by different companies from Kelly's to Whites, Pigots or Wrightsons and the Post Office, which cover the late 1700s right through to the twentieth century. Within these volumes are illustrated adverts, a detailed history of the town, and a list of churches, schools and official buildings. A street directory in alphabetical order lists the main occupier at a property. But if you want to search for a specific person, the next section lists all names in alphabetical order with their address. In another section trades are listed in alphabetical order, with each individual involved in that trade entered alphabetically, and then a list of tradespeople in alphabetical order with their address and trade.

Some directories have been digitialised and appear on Ancestry.co.uk under the title 'Midlands and Various UK Trade Directories', and can either be searched by name or you can choose to browse a particular volume. Again, very much like browsing through newspapers, you can get sidetracked by all the other information you can find in them.

Electoral Registers

In 1832 the Representation of the People Act introduced a new way to elect a government and introduced the electoral register. Of course, you won't find your lower-class ancestors on the electoral rolls but if you do find an ancestor you will know he was reasonably wealthy. Up until 1867 only men with property worth £10 could vote, after 1867 this figure was dropped to £5. Also in 1867 those who occupied land and paid an annual rent of at least £50 could vote. In 1884 anyone who owned a dwelling house could vote, along with someone who paid rent of £10 or more.

After the First World War all men over the age of 21 were allowed to vote and women aged 30 or over, or who owned property, or were married to someone who did, could vote. Ten years later, in 1928, all women over the age of 21 could vote.

The electoral registers for Birmingham are available in the Library of Birmingham but they are also available online at both Ancestry and FindMyPast depending on what years you are looking for.

Land Tax Assessments

Before the electoral register we have the Land Tax Assessments, which were introduced in 1692 and continued until 1963. The tax was levied annually on land owners and, after 1772, on tenants and occupiers of property. This doesn't include labourers' cottages and such-like, only the more wealthy tenants. They were administered locally and once again, like other records, their survival varies from place to place so it is just a case of searching the indexes to see what is there for the dates and parish you are interested in. Also remembering that some, such as King's Norton, Yardley, etc., may be held at The Hive in Worcester.

Between 1780 and 1832 they were used to establish who was entitled to vote so duplicate copies were sent to the clerks of the Justices of the Peace. So if none can be found among parish records you may find some among the quarter sessions. With the introduction of electoral registers in 1832 it was no longer necessary for a duplicate copy so once again the chances of that one copy having been lost is quite probable.

Basically they give you the name of the owner, the name of the occupier and the amount they paid. You don't get the name or address of the property, so you won't know exactly where in the parish someone lived, but you will be able to ascertain who all the wealthy landowners were and who their tenants were.

Hearth Tax

The Hearth Tax was in operation between 1662 and 1689 and was a tax on chimneys. At that time it was just an excuse to raise additional revenue. The owner of a property was taxed at 2*s* per hearth and it included houses considered to be worth 20*s* or more per year. It was quite common for houses around that time, some still visible today, to be built with tall chimneys as a sign of wealth. Some even had ornamental chimneys built on the roof just to give the appearance they had more hearths in their property than they actually did have. Those who thought they weren't eligible had to provide a certificate signed by the vicar, the churchwardens or the overseers of the poor.

The tax was collected by the manor constables and passed on to the High Sheriff to be sent to the Exchequer. They were collected twice a year, on Lady Day (25 March) and Michaelmas (29 September) at 1*s* per hearth each collection day.

Again, if you find some Hearth Tax records have survived they will tell you how wealthy your ancestor was and where he lived.

Enclosure Awards

Between 1760 and 1870 there were 5,000 Acts of Parliament passed relating to enclosures and these were considered a way to improve farming. With the inventions of new machinery, it was felt that a new system needed to be considered, a system that nurtured the land and improved the soil. So it was decided, for the beneficial future of farming, to do away with the old feudal system.

Awards, as they were called, were drawn up to prove historic ownership of land that had previously been considered common land and used by the whole village to farm and graze animals. When an award was given, the landowner was then allowed to enclose his fields, thus preventing anyone else from farming there, unless they paid rent.

So not everyone benefited. The poor villager lost the small strip of land he had once farmed and had to find work as a labourer for a meagre wage. Those who owned small farms found it too expensive to erect fences, so were bought out by the more wealthy farmers. This proved beneficial for Birmingham as people started moving in to look for work in its industries. There were many areas around Birmingham that were affected by enclosure, which Charles Pye wrote of in 1818, 'The waste lands about the town being enclosed in 1800 were found to contain two hundred and eighty acres, which land now lets from thirty to fifty shillings per acre.'

When searching for the awards bear in mind that they were also sometimes known as Inclosure Awards, rather than Enclosure Awards, so it is worth looking in the indexes under both. There are two types of record: the award and the plan. The plan shows the parish map with its fields numbered. The award shows who owned that particular numbered item. You will also find detailed descriptions of the parish: its roads, lanes, pathways and neighbouring parish borders. Again, remember that with Birmingham being split between counties at that time you may find its awards scattered among the other record offices.

Tithe Maps and Apportionments

For hundreds of years a parishioner would be expected to make contributions towards the welfare of the church and clergy by giving one-tenth of what they grew or what was nurtured by the ground they used. This would include grain, wood, vegetables, eggs, wool, flour and such-like. Wild fowl and turkeys were exempt. However, beekeepers were included. Honey was charged by the pint and beeswax by the weight. Tithe barns existed to hold the produce.

This was how the parish had been organised since Saxon times. That is until 1836. With nonconformity becoming a way of life for many families, it was argued that they had no reason to pay tithes to the Church of England. The government agreed that this tax was very outdated and decided that payment with goods should be replaced by monetary payments. Hence the Tithe Commutation Act was passed in 1836.

Tithe Commissioners were appointed to oversee the production of both the apportionments and the maps. Three copies of each were made. One copy was sent to the Crown, another to the diocese and the other kept by the churchwardens. It is the churchwarden's copies that can be found in the archives.

Roads, canals, rivers, streams, etc. are all clearly marked on tithe maps, so comparing them with a modern-day map will give you an idea of where development has taken place over the last, almost, two hundred years. Buildings are not named but are marked as to their shape and size. Fields are also clearly defined. Both are given their own unique number and checking a number in the apportionments will tell you who owned the property. There is no real rule as to which to look at first, it is purely a personal decision as to what you find easiest. Obviously, if you are looking for a specific ancestor you will need to look at the apportionment first. But if you are just getting an idea as to the layout of the parish then consulting the map first may be the best option.

The apportionments are listed alphabetically by ownership, so if you are looking through the occupier's column you'll need to scroll through the whole sheet. It was often the case that someone rented their home from one person, then fields from someone else. So make sure you scan through the whole apportionment. The apportionments also give you a description of the plot number, be it a house, shop, garden, allotment, orchard, arable field or pasture land and such-like.

If you want to take your time browsing through the maps and feel you may come back to them on other occasions, as your family tree develops, the MidlandAncestor's shop are currently making them available to download. The cost differs depending on the size.

School Log Books

We have talked continually about our 'adult' ancestors but what about the children. Although there is not a lot to find out about them in early years, once schools were established you may be able to find out about their school life. The Library of Birmingham has many school records such as admission registers and log books, and just searching for 'school' in the index will also give you personal school books that have found themselves into the archives.

You will only find names and dates in the admission books, that is when your ancestor started school and when they left, but the log books will give you an idea of the day-to-day running of the school. Notes would be made of the pupils who received top marks in their class or if they were in trouble, perhaps for playing truant, so you'll probably only find a mention of your ancestor if they were exceptionally clever or if they misbehaved. But even if you can't find anything specific to your ancestor, if you can find the log books for a school they will tell you what school days would have been like for your young ancestor. You may get to know who their teacher was, when their holidays were and if the school was closed for any reason, such as a heavy snowfall or flooding, or perhaps some specific event that was happening in that particular district. So, again, a bit of local information to add to your family's history.

Rate and Rent Books

Although the original volumes are in the Library of Birmingham, you can find a selection of rate and rent books for Birmingham between 1831 and 1913 on Ancestry.

Again, these will help you follow your ancestor's movements between the census years and whether they could afford a more expensive property or, down on their luck, needed to move somewhere cheaper. If you had more wealthy ancestors, you can find what properties they owned. Usually the pages are in alphabetical order of each street with the columns giving the following details:

House number and whether it is a house at the front or at the back. The occupier's name and the owner's name. If there was, or was going to be, a change of occupier and what date. The description of the property, whether it was a house or a shop, or a shop and a house. The rental amount and the rateable value and the amount to be collected. If there were any arrears due or if the person has been excused or allowed a discount due to Poor Rate Assessment.

However, there are occasions when the books are not so explicit, just giving the occupier's name, address and amount to be paid.

Manorial Records

A manor was a complicated system that changed many times over the years following the Norman Conquest, so is difficult to describe. Basically a manor was a piece of land owned by one person known as the lord of the manor who leased the land out to various tenants. A manor could be any size from just a farm and a few cottages or a manor house with farms, common land and woods. Sometimes there was more than one manor in a particular parish.

The lord employed various people to run his manor, such as a steward to manage the estate. The steward was assisted by a bailiff and it was also the latter's job to collect the rents. The tenancies were arranged by the reeve and the hayward made sure all the fences were in good repair and looked after the common stock of animals. A constable maintained law and order.

There can be 400 years of manorial records available covering the 1400s, 1500s, 1600s and 1700s. But, once again, not all have survived. From what is available you will find what local laws had been passed, who had taken out tenancies and what their accounts showed. When a tenant died, the heir would have to present themselves in order to take over a tenancy, so here you get an idea of someone's date of death. And if that heir was a daughter, which could happen, very often, her married name and her husband's name would be listed.

What manorial records that are available in the Library of Birmingham can be found by searching the indexes at the usual sites of calmview. birmingham.gov.uk and TNA Discovery, or during a visit to the Library of Birmingham or other relevant archives. However, a lot of records are included in the personal and family papers of the lord of the manor, so it is also advisable to search for his name, too. The *Victoria County History* gives a good account on manors and those who held manors, so it is worth reading this section before doing any searches.

Also available in the Library of Birmingham are the court leet rolls. These give details of minor matters that were handled by the manor rather than the assize courts or quarter sessions. The hearings would be held in a relevant building before the lord of the manor and his officials.

Military and Police Records

Somewhere during the course of your research you are going to come across an ancestor who served with the armed forces. As already suggested, always ask to see any photographs that family members have, there's bound to be a soldier among them. When our men enlisted they often had photographs taken to give to their nearest and dearest before going abroad. You may also find memorial cards. If a soldier, sailor or airman was killed then his parents, or wife, sent them out to family and friends as a mark of respect.

All the records for the forces of the First World War, or before, are kept at The National Archives in Kew; however, many are available to download from their Discovery webpage. From 1920 records are available to purchase from www.gov.uk: follow the links 'Working, jobs and pensions', then 'Armed forces' and then 'Get a copy of a military service record'.

If you know which regiment your ancestor belonged to you can contact that regiment. The regiments themselves don't keep personal records but they would have details of any campaigns that took place during your ancestor's service. Many regiments have their own museums that give details, stories and illustrations of the history and life in that particular regiment.

There are records available on both Ancestry and FindMyPast and many other sites. Ancestry has the service and pension records for the First World War. However, it should be noted here that many were destroyed during the bombings of the Second World War, so you might not find what you are looking for. FindMyPast has records for the years 1760–1913.

Other sites give transcriptions of various records and can easily be found by searching 'army records', 'military' or the regiment to which your ancestor belonged.

As with all types of family history records, the information will differ as to how much of a soldier's record has survived. But an intact record will give you his date of birth, where he lived, his next of kin and his occupation. If the person he gave as his next of kin died, that name will be crossed out and another entered. His measurements will also be given, including height, weight, chest measurement, and the colour of his hair, eyes and complexion. If he had any distinctive marks, like a scar or birthmark, these would also be noted. Other details include the date he enlisted and the dates he was abroad and where, or if 'at home', that is based in a barracks in England, and if he was injured or killed. If he married while in service, a copy of the marriage details will be entered together with his children and their dates of birth. Sometimes the names and dates of birth of any siblings he had will be listed. If he was arrested or put on charge there will be dates and sentences. And finally there will be the date he was discharged and the address to which he went back. Then, if he applied for a pension, the reason and, if successful, the amount he received.

There are other records of interest such as the *National Roll of Honour* and *De Ruvigny's Roll of Honour*, which were both published after the First World War. They were produced privately and both only contain the biographies of men whose family paid a subscription for him to be included. *De Ruvigny's* is, on the whole, a publication of officers killed in the war, whereas the *National Roll of Honour* contains those from other ranks. The volumes of the *National Roll* for Birmingham are available in the Library of Birmingham, but are also available on Ancestry and FindMyPast. A free volume of *De Ruvigny's* can be downloaded from archive.org, a free internet library containing numerous historic books. If you do find an ancestor in either of these volumes you will not only find out about their life, but there might be a photograph included, too.

If you know a soldier was killed in the First World War, or the Second, you will probably find him on the Commonwealth Graves Commission site, cwgc.org. Here you will find his date of death, his unit, his rank and service number. Sometimes there will be the names of his parents, or his wife, and the address of the family home, as well as where he was buried or the memorial his name appears on.

If you're not sure if your ancestor was in the war or when, a search of the Absent Voters List in the electoral registers might help.

War memorials were erected in many towns and villages after the First World War to commemorate the dead of that place. A good site to find if one exists, or search those which do, is www.warmemorialsonline.org.uk. It is a work in progress at the time of writing, so if you don't find what you are looking for it's worth keeping it in mind.

The Imperial War Museum has many documents in its archives and has two webpages of interest: iwm.org.uk and www.ukniwm.org.uk. Searching these sites will produce many personal photos and stories that may involve your ancestor.

Generally the men of Birmingham enlisted in the Warwickshire Regiment, which had its barracks in Budbrooke on the outskirts of Warwick. It is no longer there but there is a museum dedicated to the regiment at St John's House on the corner of Coten End and St Nicholas Church Street in Warwick.

Perhaps your ancestor was in another force, the police force. There are many police records at TNA but Birmingham does have its own museum for its police force. The West Midlands Police Museum was originally at Sparkhill Police Station but at the time of writing is being transferred to The Lock Up in Steelhouse Lane, Birmingham. Its website, wmpeelers. com, offers a research service to trace records. However, once again a search in the newspaper index using your ancestor's name will probably bring up lots of reports regarding any cases he was involved in.

4

Compiling and Writing your Family History

As your research increases you will need to keep it in some kind of order and there are many different companies offering genealogy software to help you. It really is a matter of choice as to which you choose, all you can do is read the reviews for each and decide which feels better for you. Or you may want to go for one of the genealogical websites where you can add your details to their database. Here you can choose to share your tree with other people or keep it private, only allowing contact by the site's messenger service. Whichever you decide, the best advice is that once you have installed your software or opened a database, keep it up to date. Every time you have done some research, add it to your records; it's surprising how quickly it can get out of hand and you wouldn't want to lose any vital details.

Perhaps you don't want to use any computer software or a website. If that's the case, get yourself plenty of paper and folders. Use different folders for each family and one sheet of paper per ancestor, although this will probably expand on to another sheet of paper, and perhaps another. But whatever you choose, you will at the end of the day soon find your own preferred way of keeping your research safe, neat and tidy.

Of course, the benefit of using computer software is that you can print multiple copies of a family history to give out to other relatives. But perhaps you want to go one step further than that; perhaps you would like to publish it all in a book. This may sound daunting but really self-publishing nowadays is very easy. Of course, you might have such an exciting story to tell about your family that you are able to find a publisher who helps take out most of the complicated work and publishes and helps market it for you.

But first you have to get it all written down.

You now have two options. You can write the history of your ancestors giving their dates, the places they lived, their occupations and what that involved, including all the events which were going on around them. Or perhaps you have an interesting ancestor or an incident that happened to one of your ancestors or their family that you can turn into a novel. Maybe there are even various incidents that could become short stories and published into one book, basically turning fact into fiction.

This may seem very daunting but as long as you go about it methodically it can become a very pleasant task. Preparation is very important. First, gather together all the information you want to use, including all the documents and photos you would like to use as illustrations. Look at all your branches and decide whether your book is about just one branch, or are you going to write about just your paternal side, or just your maternal side, or both. Now decide how you are going to separate them in the book. Bear in mind you may still be continuing with your research (remember, a family history is never finished), so be practical and plan on what you already have. Don't start adding things when you're half-way through, as that might mess with the structure you have already planned. And don't think, 'When I've found that out, I'll add it.' Just forget about it and concentrate on what you have, or leave writing the book until you've found it.

Decide how many branches you are going to include. Keep it even. If every branch you have goes back four generations, ignore the other four generations you've got back to on your maternal grandmother's branch. Unless on thinking about it, you would prefer to write a book for just those eight generations. This is the decision you have to make at the beginning and then stick to it.

Are you going to write it in chronological order? Is each chapter going to be a separate family or a separate period of time, perhaps even one generation per chapter? Or are you going to use the towns they lived in as separate chapters – all the family who lived in one town in one chapter, with a history of the town too, and then a new chapter for another town and another set of ancestors?

Perhaps you want to just cover a certain period of years. Perhaps just one hundred years to include all your ancestors who have lived during that period. Here you'll need to find a starting point – the birth of an ancestor or an event in history. Then go forward or back one hundred years.

Don't forget, this shouldn't be just a family history of dates and names; include pieces of history that were happening in the years your ancestor lived. Try to imagine what your ancestor may have looked like. How did their occupation affect their appearance? Were their hands the hands of a manual worker or did they only do light work? Were they wealthy? If so you will already have seen a copy of their will, so can show what property and amount of money they had. Perhaps an inventory was attached to the will so you can describe their house. Or were they struggling and needed help from the overseers? If so then describe the amount of times they visited the vestry and whether they were successful or not.

Think about who is reading the book and write as if you are talking to them. Probably the only people who will read it will be other members of your family, or perhaps contacts you have made during your research who are distant relatives. However, you could always give a copy of your book to the record offices or libraries local to the area in which your ancestors lived, making it available for future researchers. But perhaps the best people you can imagine you are telling the story to are your grandchildren and your great-grandchildren. Write it for them and imagine you are talking directly to them and those descendants you haven't met yet.

Perhaps you would like to write everything down as if your ancestor is doing the talking. If so, what questions would you ask them and what do you think their answers would be? Ask them to describe where they live, who their neighbours are – the census can give you that answer. How their type of work has changed over the years, with new inventions and working conditions. What world events are happening or have happened in their lifetime. Although your ancestors are doing the talking, you can find those answers from history books, but to make it personal just write it as if your ancestor is doing the talking. Perhaps you could write as if they are reading an article from their favourite newspaper; if so, utilise the newspaper archive to find a relevant article.

You may find you're not able to write the same amount for each generation. Remember, all families are different and each individual may have done more than another. But don't worry, you can always 'fill in' by going a little 'off track' and writing about something that is going on around them. Perhaps a neighbour has done something interesting that they would have been interested in or talked about among the family.

Writing your book as fiction may be a daunting task but if you have the material just follow your heart and the story will unfold. We all have our own styles but all you need is an idea and a good knowledge of punctuation and how to phrase sentences.

So what ideas could come from family history? You'd be surprised. Something quite simple could trigger an idea and then all you need is your imagination.

You discover an ancestor had quite a large property but you find he and his wife both came from poor backgrounds, so you wonder how they could have progressed so quickly. It was probably by just working hard but it could turn into a story. You know their eldest daughter was born before they were married, so there could be a possibility she is not the husband's daughter. Did he marry the mother to give the daughter a father? Perhaps he had loved her mother for some time but she had had an affair with a local landowner. And when this local landowner died he left the family something to give his daughter a secure future.

So the story unfolds. You see the couple playing together as children, growing up together. She goes to work at the 'big house', where one of the sons seduces her. Obviously he refuses to marry a young servant girl and she gets thrown out by his mother, who doesn't even know the child belongs to her son. But later, much later, the son confesses to his father, who makes provisions for his grand-daughter. And everybody lives happily ever after.

When your book is completed you now have the decision of how you are going to publish it. Of course, this will depend on how many copies you want to be made available. This will determine if you want to use a self-publishing company and just have a few copies printed off, whether you want to use many of the companies that publish on digital platforms, or whether you want to make the rounds of the traditional publishing houses. The decision is yours and there are lots of choices by searching the internet.

★★★

During the previous chapters, a lot has been said about the websites of Ancestry and FindMyPast, mainly because these seem to be the most popular with family historians. However, there are many other useful sites that are easy to find on the internet and which you, yourself, might prefer to use. But once again, for the benefit of all the hardened family historians out there, please use digitised records or if you only find a transcription find some way of viewing the original record for authenticity.

So to end on a family history conundrum: a song written in 1947 by Dwight Latham and Moe Jaffe. Entitled 'I'm My Own Grandpa', it has been recorded by many artists including Ray Stevens, Willie Nelson and The Muppets:

Now many many years ago, when I was 23, I was married to a widow who was pretty as can be.
This widow had a grown-up daughter who had hair of red. My father fell in love with her and soon they too were wed.
This made my dad my son-in-law and changed my very life. My daughter was my mother 'cause she was my father's wife.

To complicate the matter, even though it brought me joy, I soon became the father of a bouncing baby boy.

My little baby then became a brother-in-law to Dad, and so became my uncle though it was very sad,

For if he was my uncle, then that also made him brother to the widow's grown-up daughter who of course, was my step-mother.

My father's wife then had a son who kept him on the run, and he became my grandchild for he was my daughter's son.

My wife is now my mother's mother and it makes me blue because, although she is my wife she's my grandmother too.

Now if my wife is my grandmother, then I'm her grandchild, and everytime I think of it it nearly drives me wild.

For now I have become the strangest case you ever saw. As husband of my grandmother, I am my own grandpa.

5

Working in Birmingham

Of Birmingham industry, Thomas Anderton says:

> A city that produces Artificial Human Eyes may see its way to make anything; consequently, all sorts of diverse things are produced in Birmingham, from coffin furniture to custard powder, vices to vinegar, candles to cocoa, blue bricks to bird cages, handcuffs to horse collars, anvils to hat bands, soap to sardine openers, &c., &c., &c.

So you are likely to find your ancestors working in many different trades, which will lead you to many individual facts to add to your family history as to their places of work, what they did and what their working life would have been like.

So how can you find this information? The main source would be trade directories, but searching the newspaper indexes may reveal articles and reports that give details of the factory or business they worked at or their employer, any of their colleagues or perhaps your ancestors themselves. And the census not only shows you what your ancestors were doing but also what their neighbours and other residents were doing. The indexes in the Birmingham Archives will list the records they hold for many different companies. Some like Soho and Cadbury's are huge collections. Others may be just one document that has found its way into a bundle handed over with some family papers, or another company's records, or documents belonging to a firm of solicitors.

It was the Industrial Revolution that put Birmingham on the map, as *Kelly's Directory* of 1872 tells us:

> Birmingham is one of the great towns of Europe, the capital of the midland shires, and emporium of the mechanical arts. The people of Birmingham have attained supremacy in many branches of manufacture, with which they supply not only England but the world. Its progress has been very much facilitated by the exertions of the distinguished men who have been connected with its history – John Wilkinson, John Wyatt, John Baskerville, Dr Priestley, Watt, Boulton, Eginton, Murdoch, and many others, by whom the manufactures of Birmingham have been improved and extended. The manufactures of Birmingham and its neighbourhood are on a vast scale, and are of the most interesting character, exhibiting the greatest proofs of skill, taste, and enterprise: they are chiefly in the working of metals.

A very different picture of the Birmingham of medieval times and before.

Medieval Birmingham grew slowly as a mercantile and market town. With no navigable river and the trade routes since Roman times generally bypassing the town, it wasn't until the market was established that Birmingham began to grow. It grew first around Deritend and Digbeth, where it is said the River Rea was easier to cross.

Birmingham may not have had a navigable river but it did have the River Rea and other waterways that provided opportunities for mills to operate. These mills were of different types: fulling mills for the cleansing of cloth, corn mills for producing flour and blade mills to grind the edge of tools, swords or knives. As time went on, other types appeared. In the early 1600s slitting mills divided bars of iron into rods that could be used to produce nails. In the late 1600s paper mills began to appear and in the early 1700s mills used for rolling metal into sheets began to replace the grinding mills. In 1741 John Wyatt had a mill in Upper Priory. His machine contained fifty rollers and was turned by two donkeys walking around an axis. However, with the arrival of steam the mills were faced with competition and gradually during the nineteenth century and early twentieth century they disappeared.

Agriculture played a part in the working life of the early Brummies. The district has very different areas of fertile ground, so it has been said that, apart from Edgbaston, all the manors were made up of common fields, pasture land and meadows in one form or another. As Birmingham grew it seems the outlying agricultural villages also prospered as the workers of Birmingham needed their produce and in turn their industrial waste was turned into manure. The agricultural labourer's wage was also governed by the higher wages of the industrial worker. It is said that they received, on average, 25 per cent higher wages than the 'ag-labs' in more rural areas.

Up until the mid-nineteenth century a large area of Birmingham was still covered by farmland but gradually these fields disappeared and as more and more expansion took place with housing and industry, by the twentieth century they had disappeared.

Some of the earliest items made in Birmingham were leather goods and in the 1550s there were about a dozen tan yards in Digbeth, some of which probably dated back to the eleventh century. Birmingham market flourished with the sale of these goods, in particular hides, which arrived not only from the local tanners, but from all over the country. In the early eighteenth century things began to change and by the nineteenth century the tanning vats had been covered up by houses and shops and the Leather Hall in New Street, where business had been discussed and the leathers inspected as being suitable for sale, was gone. The only leather used in Birmingham in 1849 was for the making of bellows and *Showell's Dictionary* tells us that a family by the name of Onions had been making these since 1650 and that their descendants 'keep at the same old game'.

Another industry that developed from the leather trade was saddlery and *Showell's* records in 1885, 'The trade has more than quadrupled during the last 25 years, about 3,000 hands being now engaged therein, in addition to hundreds of machines.'

The rooftops of Soho today and St Michael's Church, Soho Hill, consecrated 1855.
(Author's Photograph)

One successful saddle-making business was that of the Middlemore family, whose business was started at Holloway Head in the early nineteenth century and by the 1860s was employing 400 workers. With the coming of other forms of transport they began making bicycle saddles and opened new premises in Coventry, eventually closing their Birmingham firm in 1920.

Guns have been recorded as being made in Birmingham as early as 1630, with many being made to equip the armies in the Civil War, but it appears to be William III who helped the trade become established. It seems he complained that decent guns could only be acquired in Holland and at great expense. Sir Richard Newdigate, a parliamentary member for Warwickshire, on overhearing the conversation said that he knew of a gun maker in Digbeth. When the King was presented with one of these guns he immediately placed a large order. The trade quickly expanded and the *Victoria County History* lists the principal gun makers of the late 1600s to early 1700s as William Bourne, Thomas Moore, John West, Richard Weston, Jacob Austin and Samuel Bourne.

Another notable gun maker was Thomas Ketland, who started in the trade around 1760. Also Samuel Galton, who started in partnership with Joseph Farmer in 1770 and had premises in Steelhouse Lane. Later he moved to Weaman Street. A member of the Society of Friends, he was disowned by them because he refused to give up his work as a gun maker, saying that he, his father and his uncle had been in the business for seventy years.

The manufacture of guns seems to have centred around an area in Digbeth that soon became known as the Gun Quarter. In 1815 there were over a hundred businesses involved in the gun trade but by the 1830s this figure had risen to nearly 500. Then in 1851, according to the census of that year, nearly 3,000 people worked in the trade.

There were many different types of workers employed in gun making. There were the stock makers, the barrel welders, barrel borers and grinders, filers and stampers, polishers and engravers, all of them working in individual workshops. The barrels were made by rolling out two metal sheets, either steel or iron, and joining them at the edge by forging them to an immense heat. The stocks were mainly made from either beech or walnut, the military preferring walnut. The walnut wood was mostly imported from Germany and Italy, and it was said that during the Crimean War one of the principal saw mills in Turin used nearly 10,000 trees.

The only part of a gun not made in Birmingham were the locks. They were brought in from the Wolverhampton and Bilston areas.

The Birmingham Small Arms Company opened in 1861 and was the coming together of a group of individual gunsmiths. They bought a large piece of ground in Small Heath and had a factory built there. The road leading to this factory became known as Armoury Road.

The Proof House in Banbury Street was 'established for public safety' (according to the inscription over the door) and began operating in 1813. It was created by an Act of Parliament to ensure the quality of a gun. Previously to this there had been a building in Bagot Street where a group of professionals were employed to visibly inspect the guns for any sign of faults. Now, using a safe room in the Proof House, the gun would be fired using an overloaded cartridge, causing it to be exposed to a pressure to which it wouldn't normally be exposed. If it suffered no damage it would be given its proof stamp. Large guns were tested on a shooting range in Bordesley.

Considering that guns have been manufactured in Birmingham for so long, it is not surprising that ammunition was also manufactured in abundance. There was Kynoch and Co., which was established in 1863 by George Kynoch, a Scotsman, who had previously worked for Pursall and Phillips. His premises at Witton covered over 20 acres and employed a few hundred workers, the majority of whom were women. Others included the Birmingham Small Arms and Metal Co., at Adderley Park Mills and the National Arms and Ammunition Co., at Small Heath.

According to the *Victoria County History*, 'the founding of Soho is often taken as a convenient starting point for the Industrial Revolution. It certainly starts the beginning of modern Birmingham.'

John Langford also writes of the virtues of Soho, 'One of the most important undertakings, not only to the trade and prosperity of Birmingham, but to the trade and prosperity of the civilized world, was the founding of Soho by that great man Captain of Industry, Matthew Boulton.'

Matthew Boulton started as a 'toymaker' (the description being as a manufacturer of buttons, buckles and other such trinkets) in Snow Hill. He was so successful that he knew he needed larger premises, so the idea of having a place dedicated to industry was born. Two miles outside Birmingham was a barren heath used as a rabbit warren and the only dwelling on it was the warrener's hut. This was already being developed by Edward Rushton, who had taken out a lease in 1756 and had built a mill and small house. Boulton could see that this area would suit his needs exactly and so took over the lease from Rushton. In 1761, at a cost of £20,000, Boulton's dream was complete and featured spacious workshops, all connected to each other, which could accommodate up to a thousand workers.

As Charles Pye wrote, 'and then this enterprising genius established a seminary of artists; men of ingenuity being sought after, from all parts of Europe, and patronised with the greatest liberality; thus fostered by his benevolence, they soon produced an imitation of the or molu. – These metallic ornaments in the form of vases, tripods, candelabras, etc. found a ready sale, not only in this kingdom, but in France, and almost every part of civilized Europe.'

Soho produced high-quality goods, such as plated wares that looked like solid silver, buttons, buckles, boxes and ornaments, all of which were not considered to be mass produced. New designs and patterns were introduced regularly and in some cases individual wares were produced, making them the height of value.

The *Victoria County History* tells us that, 'the visitor to Birmingham in the years round about 1770 would be taken to see, first of all, the factories on which Birmingham's worldwide reputation rested. Foremost amongst these was Soho, then employing between 800 and 1,000 people.'

It was Boulton's friendship with James Watt that really changed industry in Birmingham, as *Showell's* recorded, 'Then came the world's revolutioniser, steam, and no place profited more by its introduction than this town.' A partnership between Boulton and Watt was formed in 1775.

Boulton expanded out towards Smethwick, where he and Watt erected an iron foundry on the banks of the Birmingham canal where engines were made from 1 to 200 horsepower. John Wilkinson, an ironmaster of Bradley Works in Bilston, had been the main supplier of the cylinders for their steam engines and in turn they had supplied him with steam engines for his forges. However, following an argument over the quality of some 'pirated' engines, they sued him and went on to establish their own foundry in Smethwick.

In 1778 a mint was built and with the help of steam engines, copper was rolled into sheets through polished steel rollers and cut into blanks. Previously this work would have been undertaken by men, now the process could be done with great ease by girls. Boys of 12–14 years of age were able to work the coining machines, work that previously had to be done by strong men. And apparently their fingers were in no danger whatsoever.

Charles Pye describes the manufacture at Soho:

What is here enumerated are all of them manufactured or carried on at Soho, at the present time – steam engines of every description, and for all purposes, where great power is requisite; coining of medals, or medallions, of any size required; silver and plated articles, of every description, such as tea urns, vases, tureens, dishes, candelabras, and every necessary article to decorate the table or the drawing room; metals of every description are here rolled, to any length or breadth required; patent copying machines; fine polished steel fire irons; steel buttons; ornaments for stove grates; fenders, or any other article in steel, where taste and elegance are necessary.

A contemporary of Boulton and Watt was Joseph Priestley, a scientist and a chemist who had discovered oxygen. He had moved to Birmingham from the north, but although his scientific ideas were very popular with the Birmingham people, his nonconformist views weren't. After the Birmingham riots he moved to London.

Also in that circle was John Wyatt. A carpenter by trade, in 1733 he was working at the New Forge Pool Mill near Sutton Coldfield and it was here he worked on the development of a powered spinning wheel. After he went to work with Matthew Boulton, he invented a type of weighing machine. Although his inventions weren't tremendously successful, they sowed the seeds for other inventors such as Richard Arkwright.

Boulton died on 7 August 1809 and was buried at St Mary's in Handsworth on 24 August. The parish register entry reads, 'Matthew Boulton Esq. Of Soho in the 82nd year of his age.' Watt died in 1819 and was also buried in Handsworth on 2 September 1819.

The partnership was taken on by two of their sons and in 1810 William Murdoch joined that partnership. Murdoch was a former employee who, it was said, had walked 300 miles to Birmingham from the north to ask Boulton for employment. The business continued until 1895, when it was bought by W. & T. Avery Ltd, who had been in business in Digbeth since 1813 making scales.

Although in early times the leather industry seems predominant, evidence does show that the iron industry had its beginnings in the fifteenth century and various writings seem to confirm this. Leland, on his visit in 1538, commented on the cutlers and smiths in the town, saying, 'a great parte of the town is mayntayned by smithes'. Later another writer, called Camden, said it was 'echoing with forges, most of the inhabitants being iron-manufacturers'. And William Smith said, 'Bromicham where great stores of knyves are made; for all the townes men are cutlers, or smithes.'

By the sixteenth century it seems there were an increasing number of metalworkers in Birmingham, especially around Digbeth and Deritend. Many corn mills were converted into forges making blades and hammers. Often referred to as the greatest of the Birmingham ironmongers, brothers John and Ambrose Jennens, the sons of William Jennens, went into partnership in 1625 and developed forges and furnaces in Aston. John died in 1653 but the family fortunes increased and over the ensuing years they prospered and became members of the elite landowners of Warwickshire, living in luxury at Erdington Hall. One descendent was William Jennens, a bachelor who died in 1798 supposedly at either the age of 93 or 103. He left a large estate that was divided between various people who claimed to be his next of kin. Nearly a hundred years later there were still claimants who insisted they should also be beneficiaries to what, in 1885, was thought to be an estate of £12 million.

Iron founding could be found in all its forms in Birmingham. The White & Co. *Directory* of 1849 said:

> Every article that can cross the imagination is now cast; locks and keys, hinges with moveable joints, buttons in imitate steel, scissors, and even nails, and even needles, with various other articles in the coach and harness furniture line, which are annealed and made malleable, and converted so that they will draw out under the hammer, and harden and temper like steel, as well as stoves, ranges, saucepans, and all heavier articles.

Many of these items were made from wire and the first mill used for wire drawing was Penns Mill near Sutton Coldfield, which had previously been used as an iron forge. There were two mills here and records show that in 1578 Thomas Penn ran a blade mill and Nicholas Penn was a corn miller. Joseph Webster of Perry Barr acquired both mills in 1751 and developed them for wire drawing. They closed in 1859 and the business was transferred to Hay Mills near Yardley, where a partnership with James Horsfall saw the start of a business that has lasted to the present day. The Webster and Horsfall group are said to be the oldest surviving manufacturers in Birmingham.

The making of nails was an early trade that was still continuing in Birmingham in 1849. Whites & Co. tells us that, 'a large portion are cut by power, from rolled iron, and others are cast, or founded, from pig metal, and then annealed, or made malleable, the hammer-made nails being procured, mostly, by the merchants from country makers'.

William Hutton, in describing his arrival in Birmingham in 1741 on the Walsall road, says:

I was surprised at the number of blacksmiths' shops upon the road; and could not conceive how a country, though populous, could support so many people of the same occupation. In some of these shops I observed one or more females, stripped of their upper garment, and not overcharged with their lower, wielding the hammer with all the grace of the sex. The beauties of their face were rather eclipsed by the smut of the anvil; or, in poetical phrase, the tincture of the forge had taken possession of those lips, which might have been taken by a kiss. Struck with the novelty, I enquired, whether the ladies in this country shod horses, but was answered, with a smile, they are nailers.

Nails were produced on a large scale during the sixteenth and seventeenth centuries before the industry spread out westwards away from the centre of Birmingham. Up until the 1780s nails were handmade, the iron being first prepared by rolling the blocks of iron into sheets. The thin sheet was then cut into rods that were rolled to the required size. They were then headed and pointed by the nailor in a forge. Nailing was a small industry undertaken by families in small workshops.

Pins were first manufactured in a very basic form in about 1750 by Samuel Ryland of New Street. In those times it took fourteen different workers to produce a pin – cutters, headers, pointers, polishers to name but four. Another member of the Ryland family was a wire drawer in the High Street, so no doubt he provided Samuel with his raw material.

Made from the best brass, which had been drawn successively through holes in a steel plate, each hole smaller than the previous one, the fine wire was then cut off to the required length. The heads were made by one end being wound into ringlets and a wire was pulled into a straight length from the coil. Then the point was trimmed on a circular saw. Finally, the pins were cleaned in aquafortis, boiled in a solution of tin to produce a whiter appearance and dried in bran.

In 1785 Samuel Ryland transferred the business to his nephew, Thomas Henry Phipson, and this family became the leaders in the industry for some years, also specialising in wire-drawing at their premises on Broad Street.

Later Birmingham was to specialise in more ornate designs and by 1881 there were 729 people employed in the pin trade.

The pin trade also developed the hook and eye industry and in 1862 it was said that 800 home-workers were employed putting these items on to cards.

Hinges were first patented by Izon and Whitehurst at their Duke Street foundry in 1775 and were made of cast iron. Wrought iron hinges date back to 1840 and by 1885 Showell tells us that 'many improvements have been made in the manufacture of iron, brass, wire, cast, wrought, pressed, and welded hinges, the makers numbering over three score'.

Screws were made by hand in the early days, the thread filed by hand and the head hammered out on an anvil. Then in 1849 a machine was invented by a German clockmaker that meant screws could be made five times faster and by the early 1850s 1,500 workers, mainly girls, were employed in the trade.

Showell's describes the making of a screw:

Notwithstanding the really complicated workings of the machines, the making of a screw seems to a casual visitor but a simple thing. From a coil of wire a piece is cut of the right length by one machine, which roughly forms a head and passes it on to another, in which the blank has its head nicely shaped, shaved, and nicked by a revolving saw. It then passes by an automatic feeder into the next machine where it is pointed and wormed, and sent to be shook clear of the swaff of shaving cut out for the worm. Washing and polishing in revolving barrels precedes the examination of every single screw, a machine placing them one by one so that none can be missed sight of.

In 1865 the trade was overshadowed by just one employer, Nettlefold and Chamberlain, who had the lion's share of the industry in Birmingham with nearly 2,000 workers. Londoner John Nettlefold saw how successful Birmingham was becoming and moved to a new factory in Baskerville Place, renaming his company Nettlefold & Son Ltd. In 1854 he passed the management over to his son, Joseph Nettlefold, and, at the same time, his nephew Joseph Chamberlain, joined the firm, which then became known as Nettlefold and Chamberlain. This partnership was dissolved in 1874 and continued under the name of Nettlefold & Co. When Joseph Nettlefold died in 1881, a partnership with Guest, Keen & Co. followed and the company became known by their initials, GKN.

Nettlefolds used up-to-date equipment and also produced wire, nails and staples among other things, as *Showell's* tells us:

> In the nail mill the Paris points, as wire nails are called, are cut from the coil of wire by the first motion of the machine as it is fed in, then headed and pointed at one operation, sizes up to one inch being turned out at the rate of 360 a minute. In the manufacture of spikes, the punch for making the head is propelled by springs, which are compressed by a cam, and then released at each stroke; two cutters worked by side cams on the same shaft cut off the wire and make the point. A steel finger then advances and knocks the finished spike out of the way to make room for the next. Wire staples, three inches long, are turned out at the rate of a hundred a minute; the wire is pushed forward into the machine and cut off on the bevel to form the points; a hook rises, catches the wire, and draws it down into the proper form, when a staple falls out complete.

Metal sheathing was another successful industry in Birmingham. In April 1791 an advert appeared describing one such maker, 'By the King's patent, tinned copper sheets and pipes manufactured and sold by Charles Wyatt, Birmingham and 19 Abchurch Lane, London.' It wasn't an invention that would make Charles a millionaire but because his sheets were coated in copper, which prevented corrosion and protected the iron they were placed on, they were recommended by ship builders.

The idea caught on and other companies followed. George Frederick Muntz developed and patented Muntz metal in 1832 and manufactured it at his premises on Water Street. Five years later he moved to Swansea but then returned in 1842, buying James Watt's ironworks. The company was eventually bought by Elliotts Metal Company in 1921.

W. Elliott & Sons, metal rollers and wire drawers, first came into being in 1853. In 1862 Elliott's Patent Sheathing and Metal Company was formed, becoming Elliott Metal Company in 1874. Based in Selly Oak, they remained here until the 1920s.

The process of tinning iron pots and other hollow-ware was patented by Jonathon Taylor in 1779 as a way of making iron pots look more attractive. The concept, which was also much cheaper than using brass, was taken up by Izon and Whitehurst of Duke Street. Coupled with their hinge making, they became so successful they eventually moved to larger premises in West Bromwich.

In 1799 a Mr Hickling began enamelling hollow-wear but his process proved unsuccessful and it wasn't until 1839 that improvements with enamelling were made. According to *Showell's Dictionary*, 'Messrs Griffiths and Browett, Bradford Street, have the lion's share of the local trade, which is carried on to a much greater extent at Wolverhampton than here.'

It was estimated in 1885 that over 15,000 tons of tubes were made in Birmingham of a variety of materials: copper, brass and iron being the main components. In 1803 Edward Tomason was making tubes of iron with a brass coating. Later, in 1838, Charles Green began making seamless tubes; the design was then improved in 1850 by Thomas Attwood and by G.F. Muntz Jnr in 1852.

Boiler making began as a small trade in Birmingham but improved slowly. It seems to have started there in about 1831 with thirty men and boys working in the trade, which supplied about 150 tons a year. In 1860 the supply had risen to about 1,000 tons made by 200 workers, but twenty years later the figures had risen to about 800 workers supplying 4,500 tons.

Brass items were being made in Birmingham as early as 1668 but the earliest brass foundry was established in 1715 by Walter Tippin and Henry Carver. However, William Hutton tells us, 'The manufacture of brass was introduced by the family Turner, about 1740, who erected those works at the south end of Coleshill-street; then, near two hundred yards beyond the buildings, but now the buildings extend about five hundred beyond them.' Trade directories at the time state that 'the family' were a John and William Turner of Coleshill Street.

At first only small items such as pots and basins were made but after a few years numerous items went into production. In 1823 Thomas Horne invented the process of making pressed brass rack pulleys for window blinds and this process was then applied to many other items. Picture frames were made by Maurice Garvey in 1825.

The growth of the brass industry advanced during the late eighteenth century and by the mid-nineteenth century anything that could be made from brass was. From bedsteads to gas fittings, Birmingham was one of the main centres for the industry.

In 1885 *Showell's* writes that, 'in 1865 it was estimated that the quantities of metal used here in the manufacture of brass were 19,000 tones of copper, 8,000 tons of old metal, 11,000 tons of zinc or spelter, 200 tones of tin, and 100 tons of lead, the total value being £2,371,658. Nearly double this quantity is now used every year. The number of hands employed in the brass trade is about 18,000.'

In the nineteenth century brass founders used casting as the method for producing their goods; that means molten copper alloys being poured into moulds, whereas braziers made the goods by hand, shaping them from sheets by beating or hammering. The trade attracted workers from all over the country and a typical workshop in the mid-nineteenth century employed around twenty-five men, which included casters, polishers and finishers.

In James Guest's updated version of William Hutton's book he wrote:

I need not stay to enumerate the articles made in brass, both useful and ornamental; suffice it to say, that numerous as are the productions of this useful metal, they are all more or less made here. And the trade in all its branches, which time, caprice, fashion, taste, and ingenuity have introduced, cannot be out-numbered by any trade or profession in this place.

Some specialised in certain things. Alfred and Edwin Newman, who were brass founders initially and made cabinet fittings, went on to specialise in coffins. Newman Brothers Coffin Furniture Factory was established in 1894 and continued in business until 1998. It made brass furnishings for coffins that could be anything from handles to name plates.

Others specialised in candlesticks and chandeliers or brass bedsteads. R. W. Winfield's business in Cambridge Street was established in 1820 and provided exhibits for the Great Exhibition of 1851. Showell writes that:

> Many beautiful works of art have been manufactured in this town, which, though the wonder and admiration of strangers, receive but faint notice here, and find no record except in the newspaper of the day or a work like the present. Among such may be ranked the superb brass chandelier which Mr R W Winfield sent to Osborne in 1853 for Her Majesty, the Queen.

Designed in the Italian style and ornamented with the figures of love, plenty and peace, Prince Albert was particularly struck by it as he said that it was 'the finest work he had ever seen made in this country'.

Birmingham began its construction of metallic and brass bedsteads in the 1830s but it took some time before the industry grew. By 1850 there were only four or five manufacturers producing about 500 bedsteads a week. By 1862 there were twenty manufacturers employing around 2,000 people.

Metal bedsteads became fashionable in the 1840s. Until the 1800s beds had been made of solid wrought iron, which were expensive to make as the joints had to be joined together by forging. Then came the discovery that it was possible to use dovetail joints. The first to use this method in Birmingham was Preston, Hoyland & Peyton, which later became Hoskins & Sewell. Based at their Bordesley Works, they went on to make hospital beds for the NHS.

Birmingham could provide all the components: steel or brass for the frames, iron for the castings and wire for the mattresses. The mattresses were made by women and young girls.

Benjamin Cook of Whittal Street discovered the process of making articles of furniture with rods of iron covered in brass or other metals. He later went on to produce bedsteads of metallic tubes covered in papier mâché and then ornamented them using the japanning process or by painting, gilding or varnishing.

Other bedstead makers were Edward and Henry Peyton of Bordesley, who took out a patent in 1850 and continued in business until 1884, and R.W. Winfield, who diversified from chandeliers. John and Joseph Taunton of the Belgrave Works on Sherbourne Road started in 1896 and continued into the 1930s. Samuel Whitfield & Sons started at the Viaduct Works on Oxford Street in the 1860s, with S.B. Whitfield & Co. continuing the business at the Gladstone Works, Watery Lane in 1881. The Atlas Works on Broad Street began in the mid-1880s and continued until 1958. The factory was demolished in 1986 and the Sea Life Centre now stands in its place but a blue plaque here commemorates Birmingham's involvement in the bedstead industry.

William Hutton wrote that 'the manufacture of iron, in Birmingham, is ancient beyond research, that of steel is of modern date'. Steel had been introduced into Birmingham by the Kettle family in the early seventeenth century and their furnaces, converting iron into steel, gave its name to Steelhouse Lane.

Sword blades were made from the best-quality steel available and the worker had to gain a considerable skill to forge them into a quality that enabled them to stand up against what they were put through. Each sword underwent a rigorous test. First both edges of the steel were struck on a cylindrical block of wood, then the sides were stuck on a flat slab of hard wood. One end was placed between two bars of iron and a hand wrench fixed at the other end until the point stood at right angles with the shoulder. If at any time the blade bent and would not recover its shape, or even broke, it was returned to the forger. It was possible that a bad lot of steel had been used, so sometimes it wasn't the only one from that batch to break. Between the French Revolution and 1814, business in Birmingham boomed and many made their fortunes but then many lost them when peace came in 1814.

Without steel, many of the 'toys' that were made in Birmingham wouldn't have been made. Birmingham was long known as 'the toymaker of the world', which here refers to items such as tools, buckles, buttons, snuff boxes and other such items. As Anderton says:

> When in the winter season I see skates prominently exposed for sale in our shop windows I am reminded of another of the old or rather side industries of Birmingham. I refer to the steel toy trade. The word toy seems appropriate enough when applied to skates and quoits, but seems a curious word to designate such articles of distinct utility as hammers, pincers, turnscrews, pliers, saws and chisels, yet these articles and many others of a similar kind are included in the words steel toys. This steel toy trade, if not a great industry in Birmingham, is an old-established one, and has been carried on for years by good well-known local names, such as Richard Timmins and Sons, and Messrs. Wynn and Co., and others.

In the 1700s snuff taking was very much a fashionable pastime, so the manufacture of snuff boxes gave employment to a large number of people in Birmingham. In *Showell's Dictionary* it is mentioned that, 'one of these workmen it is recorded that he earned £3.10s per week painting snuff-boxes at ¼d. each'. The mention of snuff boxes being made in Birmingham is first recorded in 1693 but by the early nineteenth century Birmingham was developing a successful business in the making of snuff boxes. Manufacturers such as Edward Smith, Nathaniel Mills and Samuel Pemberton specialised in rectangular shapes, which were decorated with castles or abbeys.

The Pemberton family dates back to the early 1600s, when Thomas Pemberton was a goldsmith. A hundred years later John Pemberton was a wealthy iron founder. Then three generations of Samuel Pembertons worked as silversmiths and jewellers.

When the use of snuff died out many snuff box makers, including Nathaniel Mills, continued their business by making silver vinaigrettes and engraved visiting card cases.

Buckles became fashionable as shoe fasteners during the reign of Charles II, but could also be found on other accessories such as hats, so were made in all shapes and sizes. Prices varied too, from some just costing a few pence to others being a guinea a pair. An efficient buckle maker often bragged at being able to make a thousand buckles a day.

In 1788 there were an estimated 4,000 workers employed in the buckle industry in the Birmingham area, according to James Luckcock writing in the *Birmingham Chronicle* in February 1824. Ten years earlier, a new way of plating had been introduced that had changed the prosperity of the buckle trade. Casting the buckle in silver, using specially prepared moulds containing an additional mixture of tin and other metals, made the buckle harder and more durable, and more attractive to the eye.

The introduction of shoelaces in the early 1790s naturally caused problems for the buckle makers and some even caused riots, pushing the wearers of laces and even robbing them. Petitions were sent to the Royal Family asking for support.

In *A Century of Birmingham Life*, John Langford wrote, 'Great consternation was caused at this time among thousands employed in one of our important stable trades. A change of fashion threatened to banish the far-famed buckle. The manufacturers and artisans were naturally alarmed, and the practice of tying shoes was declared to be "unmanly, absurd, and ridiculous".'

Hoping for royal intervention, several buckle manufacturers from Birmingham and neighbouring towns went to London to seek an audience with the King, whereupon he promised them that he and his household would not use shoelaces. His brother, the Duke of York, also agreed to cooperate with his brother.

However, buckles did go out of fashion but when they did, buttons became more fashionable and now Birmingham came into its own.

Showell's tell us that, 'The earliest record of button-making we have is dated 1689, but Mr Baddeley (inventor of the oval chuck), who retired from business about 1739, is the earliest local manufacturer we read of.'

Buttons have always come in different shapes and sizes: round, oval, square, pea and pyramid were all mentioned by William Hutton in 1783. The cost of buttons also seems to have come in a variety of prices, as James Guest elaborates in the 6th edition of Hutton's *History* in 1836. He mentions figures of 3*d* a gross to, an unbelievable, 140 guineas. They also came in a variety of materials: glass, porcelain, horn, bone, pearl, iron, brass, hard whites (a mixture of zinc and a small amount of copper) and gilded metal, or Bath metal (a larger proportion of copper and a small amount of zinc), papier mâché and leather. The most expensive were hand-cut and polished in steel to sparkle like diamonds, and they cost nearly as much as diamonds. The cheapest were made on simple lathes or stamping machines.

Glass buttons were often made with coloured tinsel or foil placed at the back to make them look coloured and set in a thin brass frame. However, it seems the glass button wasn't popular in Britain, so was mainly exported. Horn, bone and pearl buttons were popular, but it seems, certainly in the early 1800s, that iron buttons were both the most popular and easiest to make. They were made to look like imitation bone by annealing them so a little of the rough edge was taken off. This process was achieved by placing a number of buttons in the cylindrical box so they actually smoothed each other. Sent to the japanner, they were given a coat of black varnish and were then ready for sale. It was said that one man, helped by two boys, could make four to five hundred dozen a day.

Gilt buttons became fashionable as the buckle industry was failing and by the late 1700s about 4,500 people were employed in the making of gilt buttons. Cheaper than plating, the makers of plated buttons began complaining of fraudulent activity and an Act was passed protecting the platers and inflicting heavy fines for anyone suspected of producing fraudulent copies, although really in the end it was just accepted as competition. It was

something many crafts people of Birmingham were always fighting over –
competitors who answered to the demands of the mass market.

However, Acts were passed during the 1700s to prevent the import
of foreign buttons, made of hair or covered in fabric. Any tailor using
such buttons would be fined, as would anyone wearing clothes featuring
this type. Eventually cheaper imports did come into Britain from other
countries, so sadly the gilt button industry in Birmingham started to fail.
Showell's noted that:

> The gilt button days of Birmingham was a time of rare prosperity, and dire
> was the distress when, like the old buckles, the fashion of wearing the gilt
> on the blue went out. Deputations to royalty had no effect in staying the
> change, and thousands were thrown on the parish. Sixty or seventy years
> ago there were four or five times as many in the business as at present, blue
> coats and gilt buttons being in fashion.

In 1778 Henry Clay brought out a patent for papier mâché buttons, which
became popular. He also made buttons out of slate. The first steel buttons
with facets were introduced by Matthew Boulton and it is thought that
some were of such superior design he received as much as 140 guineas for
a gross. In the early 1800s other types were introduced – horn buttons,
Maltese buttons (made of metal and glass beads), white metal buttons and
Bath metal drilled shank buttons.

In 1837 William Elliot began designing fancy silk buttons and Humphrey
Jeffries began making three-fold linen buttons in 1841. For a time cloth
buttons became immensely popular and a report in 1864 suggested that in
order to produce these buttons just one firm required 63,000 yards of cloth
and 34 tons of metal.

The shells for the making of pearl buttons were collected from all over
the world: the East Indies, the Red Sea, the Persian Gulf, the islands in
the Pacific Ocean, Panama, and the coastlines of Africa, Central America,
Australia and New Zealand. In 1885 there were 265 button makers in
Birmingham, 152 of them were pearl button makers, the rest being made

up of those producing buttons made from horn and bone, glass, ivory, gilt metal, wood, linen, brass and silver.

Of all the renowned 'toymakers', probably John Taylor is the most celebrated. Of him William Hutton said, 'we owe the gilt button, the japanned and gilt sniff-boxes, with the numerous race of enamels', adding that he was an 'uncommon genius' and that he was 'the Shakespeare or Newton of his day'. Langford also spoke of him saying, 'he was, indeed, a skilful, ingenious, and successful manufacturer; and the importance of the button trade to the town may be seen from the fact that, in the historian's (Hutton) time, in his shop were weekly manufactured buttons to the amount of £800.'

John Taylor was born in 1711 and started as a cabinetmaker but then turned to manufacturing buttons, buckles and snuff boxes in his factory in Union Street. An entrepreneur in the professional world of his day, his business went from strength to strength. He invested in land and property and in 1768 bought Moseley Hall in Yardley. Together with Sampson Lloyd, an iron manufacturer, he set up the Taylor & Lloyd Bank in Dale End, which went on to become Lloyds Bank. When he died in 1775 he was worth £200,000, a lot of money in those days.

In 1900 Thomas Anderton wrote that:

One quarter of the city – the Hockley district – is chiefly devoted to what cynical people call the production of baubles. If anyone doubts the extent to which the jewellery trade is carried on, and the number of hands engaged in it, let him station himself somewhere Hockley way at the hour of one o'clock in the day, and he will see for himself. No sooner has the welcome sound of the tocsin been heard – almost indeed before it has time to sound – hundreds, aye thousands of men emerge from their workshops, and for a time quite throng streets that just before the magic hour of one p.m. were comparatively quiet and empty. Curiously enough these working jewellers seem to come from hidden and obscure regions, and appear in the open from their industrial cells through many small doors and entries, rather than through large gateways which are opened at certain regulation hours.

The jewellery trade is not carried out in large factories with tall, towering stacks, powerful steam engines &c., Machines may be used in certain branches of the trade but, speaking generally, working jewellers sit at their bench, play their blow-pipe, and with delicate appliances and deft hands put together the precious articles of fancy they make.

But there was a time when the jewellery trade suffered a recession, as told in *Showell's Dictionary*:

A deputation from Birmingham waited upon Prince Albert, May 28, 1845, at Buckingham Palace, for the purpose of appealing to Her Majesty, through His Royal Highness, to take into gracious consideration the then depressed condition of the operative jewellers of Birmingham, and entreating the Queen and Prince to set the example of wearing British jewellery.

They had taken presents with them: for Queen Victoria an armlet, a brooch and earrings made by Thomas Aston of Regents Place and a buckle made by Mr Baleny of St Paul's Square; for the Prince a watch chain and key also made by Thomas Aston and a seal made by Mr Baleny. At the time 5,000 families in Birmingham were connected to the jewellery trade.

Things seemed to get worse, as *Showell's* goes on to say, 'at the present time (March 1885) the trade is in a very depressed condition, thousands of hands being out of employ or on short time, partly arising, no doubt, from one of those changes in fashion which at several periods of our local history have brought disaster to many of our industrial branches.'

Perhaps it was the number of people working in the jewellery trade that caused the problem. Directories in the 1780s suggest there was about twenty-six jewellers in Birmingham; in 1880, about 700.

An integral part of the jewellery quarter were the watchmakers, a small industry where many workers worked in small workshops, or their own houses, sometimes with an apprentice or a couple of workers. In 1885 *Showell's* lists the three leading watchmakers of Birmingham as Messrs Brunner of Smallbrook Street, Swindon's of Temple Street and Ehrardt's of Barr Street West, who did have larger premises. However, going through the trade directories of Birmingham there are numerous names listed under 'watch and clock makers'.

Before 1773 there was no assay office in Birmingham, so goods had to be sent to London or Chester for assaying and hallmarking. The delay was bad enough but the journey could also produce risks of damage and expense, and manufacturers felt that, in order to prosper, they needed an office of their own. One of these manufacturers was, of course, Matthew Boulton. Thanks to his friendship with Lord Dartmouth, he was able to lobby parliament to get an Act passed for the establishment of the Birmingham Assay Office on 28 May 1773.

With no specific building, business was at first carried out one day a week in three rooms at the King's Head in New Street. Eventually in 1816, after moving to various other places such as houses in Bull Lane and Little Colemore Street, an old Baptist Church in Little Union Street was converted. In 1877 a new building was erected in Newhall Street.

It is also thanks to Matthew Boulton that Birmingham has an anchor as its hallmark. During his time in London he stayed at the Crown and Anchor Inn. A toss of a coin decided an anchor and not a crown would be Birmingham's hallmark.

Another advocate of the assay office was Samuel Garbett, who had been born in Birmingham in 1717. As a young man he worked as an agent, buying Birmingham merchandise for a London agent, but by setting up his own agency he made a lot of profit and became a wealthy man. He then met Dr John Roebuck, a Scotsman who had a practice in Birmingham, and they set up a partnership. A factory was built in Scotland for the production of acid and they also developed an iron works there. In Birmingham they opened premises in Steelhouse Lane for the refinement of precious metals. Garbett was also very active in the setting up of the Birmingham General Hospital. When he was made bankrupt in 1782, Boulton encouraged him to rebuild his business and when he died in 1803 his estate was worth £12,000.

It is believed that Birmingham was producing coins as early as the mid to late 1600s. *Showell's* refer to a line in a verse written in 1682 by John

Drydon about the Shaftesbury Medal that reads, 'Twas coined by stealth, like the groats in Birmingham.' But he is not referring to an honest coin, he is referring to the art of coining, that is producing counterfeit money, which was a capital offence. And it seems Birmingham was high on the list of illegal money-making centres. In his book, published in the 1860s, on the history of Boulton and Watt, Samuel Smiles refers to scenes in the middle of the 1700s, 'One of the grimmest sights of those days were the skeletons of convicted coiners dangling from gibbets on Handsworth Heath.'

But not all coins in Birmingham were counterfeit. Boulton saw that a steam-operated press could make a coin much quicker and cheaper. Starting on a small scale, in 1788 he obtained a contract with the East India Company. This proved so successful that contracts with other companies, including the British Government, followed. The Soho Mint remained in operation through the early 1800s, Boulton's son taking over, followed by his son. It finally closed in 1850 to make way for building developments.

The Birmingham Mint in Icknield Street started producing coins and tokens in 1850. Originally known as Heaton's Mint, it was started by Ralph Heaton, who used the second-hand presses he had purchased from Matthew Boulton's estate when they had been put up for auction. At first coins were made for the overseas market but then in 1853 the company were given a contract to produce coins for the Royal Mint. Ten years later the Birmingham Mint was employing 300 workers.

Ralph Heaton's father, also Ralph, had established a brass foundry in Slaney Street in 1794, moving to Shadwell Street in 1808. Ralph Jnr was apprenticed as a die maker and his father gave him part of his premises as a workshop, which was situated on the corner of Shadwell Street and Bath Street. When his sons, Ralph and George, joined him the company became known as Heaton & Sons and the Heatons remained in the business well into the twentieth century.

Another innovator in Birmingham's industrial history whose career started in the Soho works was Edward Thomason. The son of a celebrated buckle maker, he was apprenticed to Matthew Boulton in 1785 at the age of 16. When his father died in 1793, Edward took over his factory on the corner of Colmore Row and Church Street and began manufacturing buttons, later expanding to medals and coins. He then became a pioneer in the use of plating and went on to produce silver spoons, sugar tongs, wine labels, jewellery and much more. Also known as an inventor, his first two attempts were unsuccessful – a fire ship that would destroy the French fleet in their own ports and a wind-powered water pump. In 1799 his retractable carriage steps caught some attention and he sold a hundred units. But it was his cork screw that really took off. A design still used today, he sold over 250,000 in the first few years. In 1832 he was knighted by William VI.

The process of plating was covering a hard wearable base, usually made of copper or brass, with a layer of gold or silver thick enough to stand up to the test of wear and tear. The smallest amount of the precious metal possible was used depending on what the plated sheet was going to be used for. It had to have a thicker coating if the item being coated was going to be machine-stamped or pressed into an elaborate shape than if the article was just going to be shaped by hand or engraved.

The main users of these plated sheets in the mid-eighteenth century were the smaller, individual toymakers: the makers of candlesticks, buttons and buckles who were not able to roll their own sheets. However, establishments such as Soho could roll their own plate. According to *Showell's*, in 1799 there were ninety-six platers in operation but with the invention of electro-plating by 1885 'their names might now be counted on one's finger ends'.

White & Co. describe electro-plating and magneto as:

among the more singular events of the age, that the accidental observation of a deposit, precipitated by the action of the galvanic battery cell, containing sulphate of copper, being a complete copy of such cell. Who would have thought, that the mere dissolving of metals by acid, or the revolving of wire in front of the poles of a magnet, should be the means of establishing a trade which is useful, most beautiful, and promises to become the most extensive the art working in metals may have to boast of.

Electro-plating was a boon to the silver industry and the pioneer of this process was George Richards Elkington. The technique had been discovered in 1846 by a surgeon, John Wright, and was taken up by Messrs Elkington's, who had already been dipping ornaments in solutions made from either gold or silver since 1838. Following this new invention, George Elkington opened a new factory in Newhall Street.

Thomas Anderton wrote in *A Tale of One City*:

> Visitors to Messrs. Elkington's are, of course, attracted by the artistic contents and triumphs of the famous Newhall Street showrooms. Those, however, who fancy that Messrs. Elkington's great and extending manufactory is kept going by designing and producing splendid vases, shields, cups, and sumptuous gold and silver services, are, of course, hugely mistaken. The ordinary spoons, forks, &c., that are seen on the tables of millions of people, are the staple productions.
>
> Electro-plating is indeed almost a magical sort of craft. How is it that dirty looking metal spoons can be put into a dirty looking bath and come out white and silvered must amaze and bewilder many strange eyes.

Another unique process that became an acclaimed industry in Birmingham was japanning, a process of painting a surface with lacquer. Almost any surface could be covered: metal, wood, leather and papier mâché.

Trays, or waiters as they were called in the 1700s, were popular japanning items. They were about 20 to 24in in length and either round, square or oval. Black trays had been given two or three coats of varnish and hardened in the stove between each coat. They were then polished with a pumice stone, then rubbed with bare hands and powdered stone. Tortoiseshell trays were only given a thin covering of varnish after being treated by the pumice stone and then, for better-quality ones, were first covered with leaf silver before being hardened in the stove. Two or three layers of Pontypool varnish was applied, which when heated in the stove became opaque. Spots were then rubbed off with a pumice stone to expose the silver beneath and once again it was put in the stove before getting one last polish.

Japanning was introduced in Birmingham in 1740 by John Baskerville. It was already an established trade in the Wolverhampton and Bilston area and over the following years was divided between the three towns. Baskerville had been born in Wolverley near Kidderminster in 1706 but by 1726 had moved to Birmingham, where he established a writing school. His house on Easy Hill included a large piece of ground and here, Charles Pye tells us, he erected a paper mill, 'in which article he excelled all his contemporaries'. He then set up his business as a japanner and this continued throughout his lifetime. However, Baskerville was also renowned for his printing works.

It was his interest in reading that led him to take up a printing press and experiment with the formation of different letters. Pye said he also beat his contemporaries in this too but that after his death 'to the disgrace of this country, were permitted to be sold into France'.

In *Showell's Dictionary* we read, 'He was somewhat eccentric in personal matters of dress and taste', and that this eccentricity continued after his death in January 1775 as he requested that he be buried in his own grounds under a solid cone of masonry. He remained there until 1821, when plans to build the canal wharf meant his body had to be exhumed, and *Showell's* continues by saying, 'his body was found to be in a good state of preservation, and for some short period was almost made a show of, until by the kindness of Mr Knott the bookseller, it was taken to its present resting place in one of the vaults under Christ Church'.

William Hutton, who knew Baskerville, wrote:

During the twenty five years I knew him, though in the decline of life, he retained the singular traces of a handsome man. If he exhibited a peevish temper, we may consider good-nature and intense thinking are not always found together. His aversion to christianity would not suffer him to lie among christians; he therefore erected a mausoleum in his own grounds for his remains, and died, without issue, in 1775, at the age of 69. Many efforts were used after his death to dispose of the types; but, to the lading discredit of the British nation, no purchaser could be found in the whole commonwealth of letters.

Four years later they were bought by a literary society in Paris for £3,700, of which Hutton said:

> We must reserve, if we do not imitate, the taste and economy of the French nation, who, brought by the British arms, in 1762, to the verge of ruin, rising above distress, were able, in 17 years, to purchase Baskerville's elegant types, refused by his own country, and expand a hundred thousand pounds in printing the works of Voltare!

Baskerville also worked with papier mâché and it was his apprentice, Henry Clay, who invented a way of making it as strong and as durable as wood. Clay worked for Baskerville in 1740–49 at his Moor Street premises and it was in 1772 that he patented the new stronger material, which could be used as panels on coaches and sedan chairs. In 1793 he made a sedan chair for Queen Caroline and from that time on was patronised by other members of the aristocracy and upper classes. By 1803 his billboard incorporated the words, 'Japanner in ordinary to His Majesty and his Royal Highness the Prince of Wales'.

He became so busy that at one time he was employing 300 workers at his factory in New Hall Street. As a japanner he introduced the use of bronze in his work. His carriage was said to be an excellent advert for his craftsmanship, with the panels made of paper and the body stripes of dark green and brown. It was pulled by a pair of cream-coloured horses.

Others followed him in the business, and Jennens and Bettridge took over his factory after he died in 1812. George Soutor introduced pearl inlaying in 1825 and Benjamin Giles other types of gems for inlaying in 1847.

Another trade that Birmingham took a large part in its development was the manufacture of steel pens and nibs. When James Guest was updating William Hutton's work in 1836 he referred to steel pens as 'a modern invention'. At first only the rich could afford a pen at 18*s* a dozen, but by 1832 they were available at 3*s* a gross and then in 1836 at 6*d* per gross.

The industry expanded in such a way that at its height as many as 18,000 pens could be made in one day by more than a hundred manufacturers. Mainly women worked in the factories; the men worked in the furnaces providing the raw materials.

The making of a 'dip' pen became an art and many became craftsmen at their jobs; at its peak there were said to be tens of thousands of varieties of pens. At the top of the trade was Joseph Gillott, a steel cutter in Sheffield who moved to Birmingham in 1821 and opened his factory in 1827. Over the years he made many improvements to the making of pens, trying out various ways of using stamping presses and other machinery. The Victoria Works opened in 1840 and in *A Tale of One City* in 1900 Thomas Anderton wrote of what visitors would see:

With regard to Mr Joseph Gillott's pen manufactory it is a very interesting showplace. Observe the steel pen emerge from its native metal, see it pressed and stamped, and again pressed and stamped, slitted, annealed, coloured, and finally boxed and packed. They can also see the penholders produced and inhale the sweet and pungent fragrances of Cedar wood, and they can look on the production of the pen boxes which are made in so many attractively coloured varieties. Female labour is largely employed – as is the custom in the pen trade – the nimble fingers and deft hands of many girls finding useful employment.

Visitors were always more interested in seeing the pens made for the upper classes, but as Anderton goes on to say:

The Graham Street works could not be kept going by merely making dainty gold pens, fine long barrelled goose quills, and other such superior productions. The everyday person must be considered and supplied with everyday pens, and the everyday person, although he buys cheap pens, is a more profitable customer than he looks. The everyday pen is so cheap that it is not used with care and economy. It is lightly thrown aside often before it is half worn, and is often objurgated and wasted because it is dipped into bad ink. But what does it matter when you can get a gross of pens for just a few pence.

Not long after this the Birmingham pen industry went into decline following the invention of the biro, and now Anderton introduces another different industry:

There are also in Birmingham certain trades that without being large industries have taken fixed root in the locality. For instance, there is the glass trade, which employs a good few men. If I remember rightly Rice Harris's glass works had one of those large old-fashioned brick domes that I fancy are not constructed nowadays. One or two, however, still remain, and I for one feel glad that Messrs. Walsh and Co., of Soho, allow their dome to stand where it did, just as a landmark and to remind me of pleasant bygone days.

The manufacture of glass in Birmingham began in the mid-1700s. The first known glass house was set up by Meyer Oppenheim in Snow Hill in 1762 and mainly supplied the raw material to other trades. When he moved to France, a relation, Nathaniel, continued the business until the end of that century.

Thomas Ostler started in the glass trade in 1807 by making small glass trinkets before progressing to chandeliers at his factory in Broad Street. He was said to have produced some of the most beautiful pieces in glass fountains and candelabras. In 1831 his son, Abraham, took charge of the company and from then the business flourished and the future generation safeguarded the company by becoming involved in Faraday's light fittings. They then continued through most of the twentieth century before being taken over by Wilkinson's.

Isaac Hawker established himself as a glass cutter in 1777 in his small glass house at the rear of his shop in Edgbaston Street. The business expanded when his son, John, built a larger glass house on Birmingham Heath. When John died in 1805 his sister, Sarah Bedford, benefited from his estate and her son, Isaac Hawker Bedford, continued the business.

The first pressed tumbler was made in 1834 by Rice Harris of Sheepcote Street, and in the 1850s George Bacchus & Sons were renowned for making cameo glass with thin layers of different colours and cut glassware such as paperweights. Another form of glass, the mirror, was manufactured by Messrs Hawkes's of Bromsgrove Street and they were said to be 'the largest looking-glass manufactory in the world', employing more than 300 workers.

In 1773 a mechanical process was discovered whereby glass could be painted using oil colours and stained glass was born. The expert in this field was Francis Eginton. He went on to supply the windows for Salisbury and Lichfield Cathedrals plus St George's Chapel in Windsor, to name but a few. Locally he made the east window for St Paul's Church, Birmingham, and the east window in the south aisle in St Peter's and St Paul's, Aston. It is thought, though, that he wasn't the first of his kind. A window in Hagley Church was said to have been painted by a Birmingham man in around 1756 whose name is unknown.

There were others who followed in his footsteps. Robert Henderson started his work in 1820 and John Hardman began in 1837 in Paradise Street before moving to Great Charles Street and then Newhall Street.

Charles Pye wrote in 1818 that:

At the top of Digbeth, very near the church-yard of St Martin's, there is a never-failing spring of pure soft water, wherein is affixed what is called the cock pump; which being free to all the inhabitants, it is a very common thing to see from twelve to twenty people, each of them with a pair of large buckets, waiting for their turn to fill them, and this in succession through the whole day. From this very powerful spring there is a continual stream that runs through the cellars, on each side of the street, and several of the inhabitants have therein affixed pumps, from which innumerable water carts are filled every hour of the day.

He also wrote of a spring in Ladywell, 'This inexhaustible spring of soft water has for a series of years been encircled by a brick wall, which forms a very capacious reservoir, from whence at least forty people obtain a livelihood, by conveying the water in buckets to different parts of the town.'

Many years later, when London engineer Mr Clark was surveying the sewers for the Corporation, he discovered an unusual amount of water around Park Street and Digbeth. He decided to lease a small section of the land to investigate. Boring down 400ft, he discovered a spring in a red sandstone formation that was giving a steady flow of what seemed to be pure water. It was analysed by Dr Bostock Hill, who confirmed it was free from any organic impurities and was ideal for the making of soda water. In 1885 the well in Allison Street was being used by James Goffe and Sons of Duke Street.

Goffe's business had been established since 1837. In the early days he had been a manufacturer of soda water and ginger beer but directories show he turned to mineral water distribution. In the early 1900s when advertising their bottled or syphoned water, James Goffe and Sons said that the water came from 'the celebrated Digbeth spring'. The advertising also said that, having become the 'Proprietors of the Digbeth spring', they planned to revive 'the old custom of carrying the water round to the public, at a charge of one halfpenny per bucket'. Anyone interested was to apply in writing.

In 1885 there were over 4,000 workers involved in making tools for other workers. Tools from pocket knives to scissors, cleavers to scythes, spades and hoes, axes and hatchets and more were all made from different patents and different designs.

Richard Timmins was a steel toymaker producing anything from tools to corkscrews. He started his business in Hurst Street in 1792 and his three sons joined him in 1821. They had a number of shops and warehouses in Hurst Street, then in 1851 moved to Pershore Street. The company ended with the death of the last son, Samuel, in 1887 and was bought by Wynn & Co. They specialised in adjustable spanners and wrenches. Wynn & Co. had begun trading in 1813 as edge toolmakers in Exeter Row, Suffolk Street, moving to Commercial Street in 1872. When they bought Timmins & Sons they became known as Wynn, Timmins & Co. and continued as toolmakers until 1969.

The making of agricultural implements in Birmingham seems to have been the speciality of only half-a-dozen firms. The oldest of these was Maplebeck and Lowe, whose premises were situated opposite Smithfield Market. They set up business around 1800 and seem to have continued for over a hundred years.

The making of chocolate is perhaps not at the top of the list of manufacturers in Birmingham but it is certainly one of the most well-known and has certainly stood the test of time.

John Cadbury opened his tea and coffee shop in Bull Street in 1834 and began experiments with cocoa. He moved to Bridge Street in 1847 and it was here that, under the guidance of his son, George, who was born in 1839, the business expanded. When George took over in 1861 there were only a dozen workers but helped by an inheritance from his mother, Candia

Broad Street as it once was. (Author's Collection)

Barrow, hard work and some financial disasters along the way, by the late 1870s he had built up a business that employed 300 workers.

It was now time to expand his premises and the decision to move out of town was made, hence Bournville was born and more will be told about that in a later chapter.

Also starting in Bull Street was Alfred Bird, a qualified chemist, who had his shop there in the mid-1800s. His egg-free custard had first been made in 1837 for his wife, who had an egg allergy. Realising how popular his custard was with dinner guests, he formed his company and began making Bird's Custard. He also went on to produce baking powder. Following his death in 1878, his son took over the business, which remained a family-run affair until 1947. It was bought by the General Food Corporation, but the name Bird's is still around today.

Having tried to cover as much of Birmingham industry as possible, let us go back to the opening paragraph courtesy of Thomas Anderton, 'A city that produces artificial human eyes may see its way to make anything.'

Artificial eyes were made by Messrs Pache and Son in Bristol Street and Edward Hooper in Suffolk Street and they were not only well-known in the British Isles and Europe, but all over the world, too. An advert in 1894 for Pache & Son of 21 & 22 Great Charles Street states, 'Artificial Human Eyes made to pattern, description, or drawing. These eyes are made from the very finest enamel, are matched and fitted to such perfection, and the movement so perfect as not to be distinguished from the natural eye. They are fitted without the least pain or inconvenience, and no operation required.'

6

Life in Birmingham

So what was life like for your ancestors in the expanding town of Birmingham? Who were they, how did they live, what were their homes like, how did they entertain themselves and what did Birmingham look like as a whole? Let us first hear how various writers described the Birmingham they knew.

Thomas Anderton writes in 1900 that:

The present century has seen the rise and development of many towns in various parts of the country, and among them Birmingham is entitled to take a front place. If Thomas Attwood or George Frederick Muntz could now revisit the town they once represented in Parliament they would probably stare with amazement at the changes that have taken place in Birmingham, and would require a guide to show them their way about the town – now a city – they once knew so well. It is no longer 'Brummagen' or the 'Hardware Village', it is now recognised as the centre of activity and influence in Mid-England; it is the Mecca of surrounding populous districts, that attracts an increasing number of pilgrims who love life, pleasure, and shopping.

Perhaps the latter sentence could apply today and one wonders what he, or Attwood and Muntz, would make of Birmingham today.

Some years earlier, a writer to the *Birmingham Daily Mail*, known only as S.D.R, wrote of his impression of Birmingham when he had first arrived on the stagecoach from London in 1837. Having left Meriden behind, he had seen 'the dim outlines of the steeples and factory chimneys of Birmingham'. Then travelling up 'the wide open roadway of Deritend; past the many-gabled Old Crown House, through the only picturesque street in Birmingham – Digbeth, up the Bull Ring, round the corner into New Street where we pull up at the doors of The Swan'.

Our visitor had rented an apartment at the top of Bull Street, which was then, with regards to retail, the principal street in Birmingham and in 1837 contained 'some very excellent shops'. At the time, Mr Adkins was a druggist who, still there in 1877, had carried on a family business that had lasted almost a century. There was Mr Keirle, a fishmonger, Mr Benson, a butcher, and a shawl shop run by Mr Page, whose widow took over when he died. In 1821 Mr Hudson had opened a book shop, which after his death was taken over by his son. There was a wine and spirits shop on the corner of Bull Street and Temple Row run by Mrs Peters. And a name reminiscent even in the twenty-first century, 'the Brothers Cadbury'. At that time one, Benjamin, was a silk mercer, and the other brother, John, a tea dealer.

The High Street, from Bull Street to Carrs Lane, housed just one large building, which the Tamworth Bank occupied. The rest of the buildings were small and most were pulled down when a tunnel was being built to house a railway line into Snow Hill station. There were courts and passages that contained small houses and Westley Richards & Co. had a gun factory there. On New Street there was the Grammar School, the theatre and the Hen and Chickens pub. There was Warwick House, which 'had originally been two private houses. The one abutted upon the footway, and the other stood some thirty feet back, a pretty garden being in the front.' James Busby, a wire worker, ran his business here before the property was taken over by the Drapery Company. There were also the offices of the *Birmingham Journal* and the *Post*.

In 1837 Broad Street contained private houses, all with their own front gardens. Here, at Bingley House, the banker Mr Lloyd lived. The house was later to be demolished and the Prince of Wales Theatre built in its place. The entrance to Broad Street was narrow and bounded by a lawn with a chain fence. On Easy Row there were several large elm trees. With the increase in traffic, the lawn and its fence were removed but the trees were left. When they were removed in 1847 they were 'little more than skeletons of trees, the smokey atmosphere having long since stopped all growth'.

Going further back to 1818 when Charles Pye wrote his book *Modern Birmingham*, we find another view of Birmingham:

Notwithstanding the extent of this town, there is very little distinction between it and a village; all the difference is, its fairs and market, for the smallest town has a constable to preside over it, and this, although so extensive and populous, is governed by two constables.

The buildings in this town extend to the distance of near three miles in every direction, reckoning from the top of Camphill, and it some years back, upon a certainty, the largest town in the kingdom. This was ascertained by actual measurement, for soon after Mr Aikin published his history of Manchester, Mr John Snape, a very accurate surveyor, drew a plan of this town, upon the same scale as Mr Aikin's. Since that time, I cannot say which of the two towns have increased the most; but, if Manchester has extended its buildings with more rapidity than Birmingham, it is a very extensive place.

Whoever walks much about this town, will perceive one very remarkable circumstance: at the top of a street you ascend into the houses by a flight of steps, and in the lower part of the same street, you descend into some of the houses; this is exemplified in Edmund-street, and particularly in Newhall-street and Lionel-street.

The country for a few miles round the town is in every direction studded with houses, belonging to the opulent inhabitants of Birmingham, or of those who have retired from the busy scenes of life.

The horse roads round this town were, within memory, from the rains, constant wear, and no repair, worn into such hollow ways, that in some instances, particularly in Bordesley, a waggon, when loaded with hay, the top of it was not so high as the foot path on the side: it was at one time fifty-eight feet below the surface. There are still remaining two specimens of the old roads, but they have been for many years useless, except in going to the adjacent grounds. One of them is situated a little beyond the sign of the Bell, on the right hand side of the Worcester-road, and leads towards the Five Ways. The other begins at Edgbaston church, and continues till you arrive at the toll-gate, on the Bromsgrove-road.

About twenty yards above the statue in honour of Lord Nelson, there was within memory the market cross, from whence the roads in every direction were measured; but from some cause or other, that custom has been altered, and it is difficult to say from what part of the town some of the roads are now measured; for example the road to Walsall. This road having been considerably shortened and improved, is now considered to be eight miles distant: (it was some years back, ten miles); but from the centre of one town to that of the other, will measure nine miles; and whoever travels that road must very justly pay for that distance. The road to Stourbridge and Kidderminster is another instance where the mile stones are not to be depended upon; for the one mile stone on that road is considerably more than that distance from the centre of the town.

Showell's Dictionary described the Birmingham of 1812:

The appearance of the town then would be strange indeed to those who know but the Birmingham of to-day. Many half-timbered houses remained in the Bull Ring and cows grazed near where the Town Hall now stands, there being a farmhouse at the back of the site of Christ Church, then being built. Recruiting parties paraded the streets with fife and drum almost daily, and when the London mail came in with news of some victory in Spain it was no uncommon thing for the workmen to take the horses out and drag the coach up the Bull Ring amid the cheers of the crowd. At night the street were patrolled by watchmen, with rattles and lanterns, who called the hours and the weather.

But if we go back to the writings of William Hutton, he describes a town that had only just started developing when he first arrived:

> I first saw Birmingham July 12, 1741, and will perambulate its boundaries with my traveller, beginning at the top of Snow Hill, keeping the town at our left, and the fields that then were, on our right.
>
> Through Bull Lane we proceed to Temple Street; down Peck Lane, to the top of Pinfold Street; Dudley Street, the Old Hinkley's to the top of Smallbroke Street, back through Edgsbaston Street, Digbeth, to the upper end of Deritend. We shall return through Park Street, Masshouse Lane, the North of Dale End, Stafford Street, Steelhouse Lane, to the top of Snow Hill, from whence we set out.

To a certain degree you can still follow that route today, although some of the streets have gone. But how different it looks now with high-rise office blocks, shops and multi-storey car parks. William Hutton told us how elegant the buildings in Birmingham were and that he was surprised by the lack of thatched roofs but it seems our Birmingham ancestors were a breed all of their own and very different from anywhere else. Hutton certainly seems to paint a rosy picture:

> I was much surprised at the place, but more at the people. They were a species I had never seen; they possessed a vivacity I had never beheld; I had been among dreamers, but now I saw men awake; their very step along the street shewed alacrity. I had been taught to consider the whole twenty-four hours as appropriated for sleep, but I found a people satisfied with only half that number. My intended stay, like Obrian's, was one night; but, struck with the place, I was unwilling to leave it.
>
> I could not avoid remarking, that if the people of Birmingham did not suffer themselves to sleep in the streets, they did not suffer others to sleep in their beds; for I was, each morning by three o'clock, saluted with a circle of hammers. Every man seemed to know and prosecute his own affairs: the town was large, and full of inhabitants, and those inhabitants

full of industry. I had seen faces elsewhere tinctured with an idle gloom void of meaning, but here, with a pleasing alertness. Their appearance was strongly marked with the modes of civil life: I mixed with a variety of company, chiefly of the lower ranks, and rather as a silent spectator. I was treated with an easy freedom by all, and with marks of favour by some. Hospitality seemed to claim this happy people.

John Langford published *A Century of Birmingham Life from 1741–1841* in 1868 and used adverts, notices and reports taken from old newspapers in order to show an accurate picture. In the early volumes he gives details of the town in which Hutton arrived and names some of those streets that he perambulated. Temple Street contained a house with a walled garden, the walls being covered in fruit trees, while other houses had gardens that led out to fields.

Off Temple Street is Cherry Street, now home to a large departmental store, but in 1742 it was a cherry orchard. In Snow Hill, now the home of a railway station, there was a farm with three fields, a barn and a stable. The main railway station in Birmingham is on New Street. Langford told how the street had once 'abounded in gardens and had a country air about it', and even from his younger days he remembered a man who he regularly saw out picking blackberries that grew along the side of the road.

Edgbaston Street and Smallbrook Street, now almost disappeared under a busy ring road, car parks and hotels, were described as being 'a most delightful part of town in which to reside', with the houses having large gardens. In Deritend there was a deer park to the north of Bradford Street, and along Bradford Street was Custard House Farm, which was described in a sales advertisement as 'the house, barns, stables and other buildings, in very good order'.

St Philip's Cathedral is now situated in a very busy part of Birmingham surrounded by banks and bars. At the time Langford was writing about it, it was described as 'the New Church' and was surrounded by gardens and 'had scarcely a house to hide it from the eye of the visitor'. The nearest houses were on Bull Street, whereas St Martin's Church was surrounded by houses and shops. Broad Street, now one of the centres of Birmingham night life, was then a country road leading to gardens and fields.

Langford also includes a description of Birmingham taken from an engraving made of Birmingham in 1752 by Samuel Bradford:

Birmingham, A considerable Market Town in the County of Warwick. It is pleasantry situated on a gravelly soil. Descending on the South East to the River Rea, it is now become very large and populous, which is greatly owing to the freedom it yet enjoys, as well as the industry of the people, and their extensive trades. The inhabitants are generally of an obliging and ingenious disposition, and have the character of being sincere in their dwellings. The houses are chiefly built of brick, and the public buildings (though but few) are neat and magnificent. St Philip's Church, which is esteemed one of the principal ornaments of this town, is built of white free-stone, and has an agreeable situation. The spire of St Martin's is justly admired, and, notwithstanding it has been built several hundred years, is thought superior in beauty to most in this nation. St Bartholomew's Chapel is lately built, and has a double row of windows on each side; ye outside is plain, but ye inside is allow'd to be very handsome and neatly finished. St John's Chapel (Deritend) was rebuilt about 17 years ago. The tower is not yet finish'd, but the body of the chapel makes a good appearance. There are, besides, Meeting Houses for Dissenters. The Free-school and Workhouse are handsome, regular, pieces of building, and may be deservedly esteemed useful as well as ornamental.

When the wife of John Baskerville died in 1788, their house on Easy Hill was sold at auction. The advert for the sale in May 1788 gives a good idea of how different Broad Street looked in those times. Even in 1868, when John Langford published his book, he commented that readers would be surprised to know that such a country-type property existed at the end of Broad Street. Easy Hill was given the name on account of it being a gentle slope leading between New Street, Cambridge Street and Broad Street:

The out Offices consist of a large Kitchen, with Servant's Rooms over it, a Butler's and common Pantry, Brewhouse, two Pumps, one hard and the other soft Water, a four-stalled Stable, and Coach House, a good Garden, with Green-House, and a Garden House, spacious Warehouses and Workshops, suitable for the Mercantile Business, or any extensive Manufactory, together with about seven Acres of rich Pasture Land in high condition, Part of which is laid out in shady walks, adorned with Shrubberies, Fish Ponds, and Grotto; the whole in a Ring-Fence, great part of it enclosed by a Brick-Wall, and is, on Account of its elevated situation and near affinity to the Canal, a very desirable spot to Build upon.

It seems the idea that Birmingham was expanding rapidly was becoming established in the minds of investors and that such a house could certainly be redeveloped.

This also happened in this same decade to an area in Aston. Ashted was named after Dr Ash, who acquired a lease from Sir Lister Holt for a plot of land to the north of Birmingham. Here he built a large mansion, which in the 1780s, together with its grounds, was sold. The grounds were sold for building purposes and the house became a church.

Some years later another sale showed how, as Langford put it, 'the town was now changing from the hardware village to the industrial Capital of the Midlands'. In 1806 it was decided by officials that the old Parsonage House, which stood at the bottom of Worcester Street, was no longer fit for purpose so the property, together with its garden, was sold at auction for £5,550. This was considered an extremely high price and that the purchaser would lose money. However, albeit nearly thirty years later, in 1835 this property, having been rebuilt, was sold at auction as thirty-one lots and produced £9,159, In these times this would have been a huge investment.

The *Birmingham Journal* described the booming town centre in the 1820s:

The most unpeopled streets of a former period were now busy with life and bustling activity. From morning to night continually swept along them a busy tide, and trains of heavy carts extending for more than a mile, loaded with coal and lime, and bars of iron from the district around, stretched from one street to another and far beyond them.

On market days there was great business and bustle. Crowds of country people gazing in at windows blocked up the narrow footway at the risk of being overturned or of danger to their limbs from handcarts and wheelbarrows rolling inside the kerbstone. Ballad singers and blind beggars swarmed at every corner. Here a brawl, the sequence of the sloppings from a trundled mop in the face of a passer-by. There a crowd round some baker's horse with bread panniers occupying the breadth of the pathway and those within playing at pitch-loaf, to the danger of some unwary inhabitant. Heaps of coals lying upon the pavement from morning to night and mud heaps all around.

Burly butchers and wily horse dealers wrangling with the country folks round droves of pigs and sheep and horses in New street nearly opposite the Hen & Chickens; and fights and runaway cattle in the Beast Market from High street to Dale End. Delighted groups of idle men and

Corporation Street *c.* 1900s. A Parisian boulevard in the centre of Birmingham. (Author's Collection)

New Street *c.* 1900s. Known to have been in existence in the fourteenth century, this road also became another of Birmingham's busy thoroughfares. (Author's Collection)

women and mischievous boys crowding round the Welsh cross hooting, and yelling, and pelting the unfortunate offender in the pillory with mud, bad eggs, and offensive garden stuff; or men and lads fighting dogs at the corner, got up impromptu, in defiance of the law.

The indoor markets became an integral part of life in Birmingham for both the customer and the stall holder as this piece from the *Birmingham Daily Post* on 25 October 1867 tells:

Fish come into Birmingham every morning from all the principal eastern coast fisheries – Hull, Great Grimsby, Lowestoft, and elsewhere; and at the present time Birmingham men have their own smacks at Torbay, and have their supplies sent up to this town. It is amusing to hear the language of the salesmen, and to observe the arts put in practise by them to dispose of their goods to their advantage.

One selling a barrel of herring runs rapidly up from 10s, to 14s.6d. As there is no further advance, his powers of persuasion are put in practise – 'Going at 14s.6p. No advance – they are good 'errings, Jim, my boy, but I don't give you no warranty; no, no, I only goes by what the man tells me, and I don't know as how he tells the truth always, no more than you.' Somebody says '10s.' Salesman: 'I should think you would, but you ain't going to get it, 11s. 12s.; any advance? I wish you would stan' back there – I can't see my congregation.' A rival salesman has sold barrels successively for 11s.6d., 11s.9d., 12s.6d., and 11s.3d. In this way an immense quantity of fish is disposed of daily.

A few years later, in January 1878, another article told how:

several fish and game dealers had secured enormous quantities of turkeys, and geese, and rabbits, and these they were selling by auction, at almost surprisingly low prices. They were busy at their work too. One stout gentleman did nothing but 'knock down' the birds, whilst he kept five or six men employed in taking money and delivering what he sold.

This trader's mode of procedure was peculiar, to say the least of it. One of his assistants would dive into a huge hamper, and haul forth by the neck a turkey, swinging it round his head to display its proportions. Meanwhile the auctioneer was vociferating – 'Now, 'en; now'en. What for it? Two-and-six, two-and-a-tanner; spring another tanner; ah! Ah! Three bobs! Down he goes.' Saying these words he clapped his hands, and it was a case of looking out for yourself if you happened to be standing near.

The instant that the clap of the hands denoted that the bird was sold, the exhibitor pitched over the heads of the bystanders in the direction of the purchaser, who had to catch it as best he or she could, whilst one of the money-takers rushed after the flying bird in search of the payment thereof. Meanwhile the auctioneer was 'knocking down' the birds as quickly as he possibly could, never staying above three seconds for a bid. They were sold at two-and-three and two-and-six and two-and-nine; some of the larger ones fetching three-and-six.

Close by was a second auctioneer, driving a barely less thriving trade. This man was a pantomimist. He would vanish, with a piercing yell, head first into a hamper, struggling forth with loud cries of 'Oh! Lend us a hand – it's a breaking my back.' Then he would hold aloft – clutching it with both hands and arching his back as though he were supporting half-a-ton weight – a turkey or goose, perhaps weighing five pounds, and elicit bids for it; whilst he pretended to groan beneath the tremendous burden of its body. He paid himself well, no doubt; for the people appeared to chuckle over the fun, and– what was more to his purpose – buy the birds. To be sure, the geese and turkeys were very scraggy-looking but they sold not-withstanding, and people seemed satisfied with their bargains.

In 1900 Thomas Anderton gave a description of some of the old shops that still existed:

Walk down the Lower Priory, which leads out of the Old Square – or what was the Old Square – he will see at the bottom of the said Lower Priory, on the right hand side, a sedate and solid brick building. He will see a brass knocker on the door and a brass plate bearing the name Smallwood and Sons. This is the business house of the oldest firm of wine merchants in Birmingham, and I believe, that these premises in the Lower Priory have been in possession of the Smallwood family since the days of the Commonwealth, and further, that the present active members of the firm are the fifth and sixth generation of Smallwood and Sons, wine merchants. There is no big shop window full of bottles of cheap heterogeneous wines and spirits. If you step inside the office, you see few signs of Bacchus or his bowl, but you do see some antiquated rooms, some quaint furniture, and a nice dry, well-seasoned appearance that denotes age.

It might be thought that such a very unbusiness-looking place would be quietly draining away, especially in face of the flaring competition in the wine and spirit trade. I am, however, glad to think and know that such old-established houses in Smallwood and Sons can bear up against the levelling down processes that characterise the more pushing branches of the wine and spirit trade. There are still a fair number of people who like to buy their wine from dealers who seem to have inherited certain trade instincts and experiences, and who can be relied upon to supply what they know to be good wines and spirits, such as can be consumed with pleasure and taken without risk. The most serious form of competition that knocks the legitimate liquor trader on the head is the grocer wine and spirit selling. It may be very convenient to the public to be able to buy a bottle of wine or whiskey when they are buying their groceries, but this convenience has been purchased, I fear, at a cost that is not pleasant to consider. I fear it would not be difficult to prove that female home-drinking has been fostered by the grocers' wine and spirit licences.

Considering the pace at which Birmingham moved forward during the latter half of the nineteenth century, it is not, perhaps surprising that few shops and houses of old date are now to be seen in the chief centre streets of the city. A few remain to remind us that Birmingham has a respectable past. Chief among that old order of retails trading establishments still flourishing in our midst I may particularly mention the shop of Mr William Peasall, silversmith, &c. As many of my readers are aware, it is situated in High Street, opposite the end of New Street, and is conspicuous for its pretty quaintness and its genuine old-time appearance and origin. There are the small bow windows, the little panes of glass, that are so suggestive of the architecture of a century ago.

The adjoining premises to Mr Pearsall's, on the east side, are also old and well in years. They have been altered with a modern dickey – I should say, front – which rather hides their antiquity. There is, however, still conspicuous a quaint and curious spout-head which bears the date 1687, showing that these premises have more than passed their bicentenary.

It was Joseph Chamberlain who, during his time as mayor, changed the ambience of shopping in Birmingham, as Thomas Anderton tells:

Colmore Row was once just a country lane but became known as an affluent business address for Birmingham's professional establishments. (Author's Collection)

Victoria Square, which leads off Colmore Row, was previously known as Council House Square. It was renamed in January 1901 in honour of the Queen. (Author's Collection)

In the year 1869 Mr Chamberlain was elected a member of the Birmingham Town Council, and he began to make things spin and burn at a pace which literally soon reached a pretty high rate – sanitary improvements were promoted, the principal streets and their lighting and paving were improved, and the general appearance of the town quickly presented a change for the better. Trees were planted in some of the chief thoroughfares.

At one time residents in the adjoining counties looked down upon Birmingham shopkeepers, and would say rather contemptuously that they never shopped in this city, but went to Leamington, Cheltenham, or London to make their purchases. But we do not hear so much of that now. On the contrary, I have heard of people – even aristocratic people – who actually say that they now, for many reasons, prefer to shop in Birmingham rather than go to London. The increased number of large and important shops of the universal provider type, where they sell everything from blacking to port wine, and where you see silk mantles in one window and sausages in another.

When it was decided to adopt Mr Chamberlain's scheme and make the fine new street, land was cleared and was let on leases by the Corporation. In letting this land, agreements were made that the new buildings, when consisting of shops, offices, &c., should be so many storeys high. When, however, these tall buildings were erected, adjacent premises were robbed of light and air, and when the owners or tenants of these injured properties asked for compensation they found out, at least in some cases, that the authorities were not liable.

When the grand new street was made the traffic in the northern part of the town was largely diverted from other thoroughfares, and the consequence was that streets and passages that were once busy highways and byways were soon comparatively deserted. Shops became tenant-less, or had to be let at greatly reduced rents. Indeed, the depression of property in the localities referred to is said to have been at least thirty per cent.

Corporation Street is now one of the main shopping streets in Birmingham and was developed following the Artisan's and Labourer's Dwellings Improvement Act of 1875. The act gave Joseph Chamberlain, the then Mayor of Birmingham, the go-ahead to clear a large area and fulfil his dream of Birmingham having its own Parisian boulevard.

The scheme involved clearing 93 acres of ground with the freehold of 45 of those acres being purchased by the Corporation together with 600 buildings. Work began in August 1878 and at the time of the publication of *Showell's Dictionary of Birmingham* was still continuing:

> When Corporation Street is finished, and its pathways nicely shaded with green-leaved trees, it will doubtless be not only the chief business street in the town, but also the most popular promenade. At present the gay votaries of dress and fashion principally honour New Street, especially on Saturday mornings, Hagley Road, on Sunday evenings, is particularly affected by some as their favourite promenade.

In 1835 a French diplomat, historian and traveller visited Birmingham and commented on how unique Birmingham was. He said:

> These folks never have a minute to themselves. They work as if they must get rich in the evening and die the next day. They are generally very intelligent people, but intelligent in the American way. The town itself has no analogy with other English towns. It is an immense workshop, a huge forge, a vast shop. One only sees busy people and faces brown with smoke. One hears nothing but the sound of hammers and the whistle of steam escaping from boilers.

The politician Richard Cobden thought the social and political life in Birmingham was 'far more healthy' than that of Manchester. This he attributed to the factories being much smaller and there being 'freer intercourse between all classes than that of the Lancashire town, where a great and impassable gulf separates the workman from his employer'.

In 1801 the workers in Birmingham were mainly found in trade and manufacture. In Aston, Edgbaston, Handsworth and Harborne there was still a certain number working the land, but in the parishes of Perry Barr, Yardley, King's Norton and Northfield the majority still working in agriculture. However, within ten years things had changed, with 95 per cent of the population of Birmingham, Aston and Edgbaston working in industry. And due to the nailing community in the Northfield parish, industry had also taken over the farming population there, too. The 1841 census for Birmingham showed that 70,000 people were working in industry, mainly within the brass trade but with the button trade being a close second.

The expansion of industry in Birmingham seems to have influenced all the workers' wages. The agricultural labourer in the early 1800s living outside Birmingham received no more than £15 a year but in Birmingham he could receive 7s a week. Some even earned £3 a week. Women earned up to 7s a week and children 1s. Wages were quite high in the jewellery and toy trades. In the button industry workers could earn between 25s and 30s a week before the recession in 1811. Jobs as piece workers were easy to find and would supplement a family's earnings.

But did this employment provide a decent lifestyle? Probably not and, despite what has been written previously, it seems that as the Birmingham industrialists progressed, the working classes declined. It is said that women in particular were exploited more in Birmingham than anywhere else. On his arrival in Birmingham, William Hutton commented on the half-naked bodies of female nail workers and these scenes were still in abundance many years later. Women shared the same hard, laborious jobs in the brass trade as men. The introduction of stamping and piercing machines meant more work for women, especially young girls, who worked for lower wages than the men and therefore saved their employer some profit. Disease was rife in factories, where mercury, metal dust and fumes were numerous and an early death was commonplace in these environments.

The Children's Employment Commission Report in 1842 showed that the worst place in Birmingham was Phipson's the pin-makers in Broad Street. They had overcrowded workrooms, filthy privies, the children worked twelve to fourteen hours a day after walking up to 3 miles to work, earning only 1*s* to 3*s* a week and were frequently hit with canes by the overseers. The screw manufacturer, Ledsam's of Edmund Street, refused to participate and the commissioner couldn't guarantee to the workers who participated they wouldn't be victimised afterwards.

James' Screw Manufacturers in Bradford Street received a good report in that their workers, men and women, all worked in favourable conditions and no children were employed under the age of 14. Boulton and Watt employed no one under the age of 13 and all their employees were literate. Four other firms under the Soho label were commended. Soho also provided protection for its adult employees with the formation of Boulton's Mutual Assurance Society, which offered sickness benefits for the workers here.

Turner's button factory on Snow Hill also received a good report, so it seems there was a very mixed image of working life in the mid-1800s.

By 1863, when another inspection by the Children's Employment Commission was undertaken, it showed much better conditions and many factories were now found to be light and airy. However, the ages at which children were working remained the same. Sometimes children as young as 5 or 6 were sent out to work, and many were certainly working by the age of 10. The Factory Acts of 1864 and 1867 brought about some improvements. Only children between the ages of 8 and 13 were allowed to work, and then only half-time. However, the wording was not considered foolproof and there were loop-holes, so it wasn't really until the Act of 1901 that legislation improved conditions.

In 1871 statistics showed that the brass industry was the leading trade in Birmingham, with the gun trade coming second and the jewellery trade third. The largest group of female workers were in the button industry, with steel pen makers, second. Working hours were becoming shorter but they were still excessive by today's standards. After 1872 working only half a day on Saturdays was becoming the custom. It seems to have been thanks to the railways that hours became shorter. Railway companies wouldn't collect parcels after a certain time – so was there any point in keeping clerks and warehousemen any later?

The proportions of the dangers and disease of the earlier years were still there. Mercury poisoning may have disappeared since electrolysis had been invented but there were now the hazards of working heavy unguarded machinery in many places and the use of acid in the refineries. With their lungs having been damaged in their youth, there was a high early death rate in metal workers over the age of 45.

All these workers needed homes and those homes took the shape of the court-style back-to-backs. They were cheap to build and cheap to rent but in some cases were poorly maintained by the owner. Many of these houses consisted of just two rooms, some three, in which a family of sometimes six or more lived. Families moved constantly; you'll notice this when following your ancestors through the census years. Some moved because with a growing family they needed somewhere larger, some may have fallen on hard times and needed somewhere cheaper, while some even packed up their few belongings in the dead of night and moved elsewhere without paying their rent. But that probably wouldn't have worried their landlord – there was always someone to fill the empty rooms they'd left. And perhaps he'd get his loss of rent back by charging the new tenants a little extra.

In the 1860s and '70s many leases were expiring and this made it possible to empty older properties, many of which were considered slums, and rebuild. This was particularly extensive around the New Street and Colmore Row area and many squalid streets were cleared in order to build the new public buildings around Victoria Square. Once the area was cleared of the rundown houses they were replaced with new office buildings and shops. Buildings took on a new facade with plate glass windows and bright lights. The people were moving out of the centre to the outskirts and suburbs and it has since been said that it was at this time the centre of Birmingham began to take on a new modern look that would take it into the future and much the same appearance it has today.

Nevertheless, there was still housing in what is now the city centre, and generally of a very low standard. A series of articles, 'Scenes in Slumland', were published in 1901 in the *Birmingham Daily Gazette* by their correspondent,

J. Cumming Walters. Walters described the appalling conditions in which thousands of people lived and exposed the deputy chairman and five of the city's aldermen as slum landlords.

These articles paint a very vivid picture of the poorer parts of Birmingham at the turn of that century: 'the air is heavy with a sooty smoke and with acid vapours, and here it is the poor live – and wither away and die'. It describes the street corners where groups of men, out of work or unwilling to work, hang around. Women stand on the doorsteps gossiping with their neighbours, their unwashed children playing in the dirty gutters. Other women pass by pushing barrows of coal or can be seen washing in the tumble-down wash houses. The alleys are full of rotting garbage, the factories with their massive chimneys pouring out their fumes of thick smoke and the foul smelling canals.

Look at the houses, the alleys, the courts, the ill-paved, walled-in squares, with last night's rain still trickling down from the roofs and making pools in the ill-sluiced yards. Look at the begrimed windows, the broken glass, the apertures stopped with yellow paper or filthy rags; glance in at the rooms where large families eat and sleep every day and every night, amid rags and vermin, within dank and mildewed walls from which the blistered paper is drooping, or the bit of discolouration called paint is peeling away. Here you can veritably taste the pestilential air, stagnant and mephite, which finds no outlet in the prison-like houses of the courts; and yet here, where there is breathing space for so few, the many are herded together, and overcrowding is the rule, not the exception. The poor have nowhere to go.

And where were these places? The writer tells us that walking around Vauxhall, Duddeston, Nechells and Gosta Green for two hours, the reader will witness these sights in all the streets. And the only place laughter is heard is in the taverns, however dingy they are, they are still full, 'what wonder that drink becomes a second refuge.'

St Martin's Church, known as the parish church of Birmingham. (Author's Collection)

THE CATHEDRAL. BIRMINGHAM.

St Philip's Church, which became Birmingham's cathedral. (Author's Collection)

One family our writer met was a woman aged about 40 who had a family of eight children. Her husband's wages never amounted to more than 18*s* a week and the family of ten lived in just three small rooms that cost 4*s* a week to rent. And they were considered the aristocrats of the street. When asked why she didn't leave she said:

> Because I can't get a house any better at the price near to my husband's place, or near the school the children go to. We've got no choice. We're obliged to take the houses we can afford, and my little children couldn't walk a mile or two every morning and afternoon and evening to their school, nor my husband to his work.

At the back of 253 Great Russell Street was a court containing thirteen houses. A year previous it had been ravaged by a fever but still there were piles of refuse and waste that hadn't been collected for six weeks. Other courts suffered the same sanitary problems. Courts in Moorson Street, Hampton Street and St George's Street were mentioned.

The reporter laid the blame on landlords and landowners, saying that not all places were the same and used two courts, No. 2 and No. 9, in Lower Tower Street as examples. The rents at both were more or less the same. No. 9 had a waterlogged yard and the houses didn't have decent windows, not that there was a decent view to look out on, only a high wall. The residents took no care over their homes but 'why should they?' asked the writer. Whereas, at No. 2, with the quality of building being in such better condition the residents took more pride in their homes, 'there is not a cracked window or a dirty pair of curtains to be seen in the place'.

Other places he named were Hanley Street, William Street North and Brearley Street, which had recently been improved. Here the residents told how they now felt respectable and as the landlord had done his part, they would do theirs.

Despite their reputation, this type of housing was still in existence in the mid-twentieth century and those who were brought up there talk of the camaraderie, the looking out for each and the friendships. One occupant who was born in 1947 says, 'I particularly recall the night soil man who emptied the communal toilet. Always thought one of the worst jobs going.'

In 1919 the Addison Act was passed, which provided local councils with subsidies to help build new homes. The first council houses to be built under this new Act in Birmingham were in Cotterills Lane, Alum Rock.

For those who were really destitute there was the workhouse, but this wasn't always the notorious place we know of from Victorian times. The early workhouses were small premises run by the parish, but when parishes were joined together under the new Poor Law Unions, larger buildings were erected to house all the poor.

The original workhouse in Birmingham was built around 1733–34 between Lichfield Street and Steelhouse Lane, with extensions being added over the following years. Hutton referred to it being like the 'residence of a gentleman'. It was extended in 1766 to provide an infirmary and then again in 1779 to provide more workrooms. It provided a home for 645 people, who could also find work there. At one time there was a corn mill or people found work spinning yarn.

In 1797 a separate building for children was opened and in the 1836 updated version of William Hutton's *History of Birmingham* we are told that:

The Asylum for the Infant Poor, established in Summer Lane in 1797, is conducted by a committee of guardians and overseers. The manufacture of pins, straw-plait, lave, &c., is carried on for the purpose of employing the children, whose labour produces a profit to the parish. There is a bath, garden, playground, school, and chapel connected with this institution. There are usually from two hundred to two hundred and fifty children in this parish family.

This workhouse closed in 1852.

After the Poor Law Amendment Act of 1834 the old workhouse in Lichfield Street continued to be used for the Birmingham Union until the early 1850s, but it had become evident in the latter years of the previous decade that a larger building was required. A site was chosen on the corner of Western Road and Dudley Road and the new building opened in 1852. Over the years it was extended and in 1888 a hospital was built on the west side. The site where the workhouse stood is now the Birmingham City Hospital.

There was a workhouse for the parish of Aston as far back as 1777. A parliamentary report listed the numbers of inmates these establishments could hold and ninety were listed for the workhouse situated on the village green in Erdington. The one in Sutton Coldfield could also take up to ninety.

When the Aston Poor Law Union was formed, it took over the Erdington workhouse and remained there until 1869, when the building of a new establishment was completed on the west of Erdington. The address was 1 Union Road (now Highcroft Road) and is now Highcroft Hospital.

In the King's Norton Union there had been parish workhouses since the 1700s. One in King's Norton stood on the south of the green and one in Harborne on Lordswood Road. In Edgbaston it was on Harrison Road and simply called a poor house. A small workhouse was established on the Bristol Road in Northfield in the early 1800s but when the union was formed it took over the building on the green in King's Norton, also keeping the Harborne workhouse in use.

Eventually these buildings became too small, so in 1870 a large building in Raddlebarn Road, Selly Oak, was built that also eventually became a hospital.

Life in the workhouse would be the last resort for destitute people and the feeling of anguish they must have felt was portrayed on the gateway into Birmingham workhouse, which read 'Archway of Tears'. A relieving officer would interview the applicant, who was initially placed in the receiving ward. Then a decision would be made by the Board of Governors during their weekly meetings as to whether the applicant justified a place in the workhouse. On acceptance, the applicant was made to undress and bathe and was then given a workhouse uniform.

Once in the workhouse, an inmate wasn't allowed out unless for extreme circumstances, such as visiting a dying member of the family. Sometimes a stay in the workhouse would be a short one, sometimes inmates regularly came and went according to their health and ability to work. Some stayed until they died. When someone died in the workhouse their family would be notified, so they could register the death and organise a burial themselves. If they couldn't, or there were no family members, the board of guardians would undertake this role. The burial would take place in the nearest burial ground in an unmarked, public grave.

When unemployment benefits and pensions were introduced in the twentieth century the workhouses gradually disappeared and the care of the poor was transferred to the local authorities. Now once again those needing help had to go before a body of men to ask for help, much like the days of the parish relief.

They could claim benefit for twenty-six weeks, which after that time sometimes was extended. Eventually they would have to take a means test and if they had anything worth selling they were told to sell it before they were given any more financial assistance. On alternative weeks they were either given their rent or a grocery ticket that had only specific items listed

Chamberlain Square as it once was. Named after Joseph Chamberlain, it lost some of its Victorian buildings and style during redevelopment in the 1970s.
(Author's Collection)

Birmingham's Council House, Art Gallery and Museum in Chamberlain Square.
(Author's Collection)

that they were allowed. There was no choice, they had to have what they were given.

As has already been said, many workhouses eventually became hospitals but there has been a hospital in Birmingham since the late 1700s. A notice appeared in November 1765 saying:

A General Hospital, for the Relief of the sick and Lame, situated near the Town of Birmingham, is presumed would be greatly beneficial to the populous Country about it, as well as that place. A Meeting therefore of the Nobility and Gentry of the Neighbouring Country, and of the Principal Inhabitants of this Town, is requested on Thursday the 21st Instant, at the Swan Inn, at Eleven in the Forenoon, to consider of proper Steps to render effectual so useful an undertaking.

The proposal was accepted and steps were taken to raise the money. At meetings in February and March the following year it was reported that Mrs Dolphin had agreed to sell some of her land at £120 per acre, which consisted of:

All those four closes, pieces, or parcels of Land, Meadow, or Pasture Ground, situate, lying, and being together near a place called the Salutation in Birmingham, containing, by estimation, eight Acres or thereabouts, be the same more or less, adjoining at the upper end or part thereof unto a Lane there called Summer Lane, and at the lower end or part thereof unto a Lane called Walmore Lane, with the Barn and other Buildings standing upon the uppermost of the said Closes towards the said Lane called Summer Lane, with all Ways, Liberties, Privileges, Hereditaments and Appurtenances to the same belonging or therewith used and Enjoyed.

Over the ensuing years numerous money-raising events took place but there never seemed enough money, so work on the new hospital was very slow. It eventually opened in 1779. As the years progressed and the population grew, the General Hospital went through many improvements, with more land being bought for expansion. It eventually closed in 1897 and the facilities were transferred to Steelhouse Lane. When the old Birmingham union workhouse became the new City Hospital, and the Queen Elizabeth hospital was built in Edgbaston, this building became the Children's Hospital.

As with all places, the Church played an important role in the lives of the people of Birmingham. Of St Martin's, Charles Pye wrote:

> [it is] undoubtedly of great antiquity, and to trace its foundation is at present impossible, tradition itself not giving a clue. It was originally erected with stone, but the exterior being decayed by time, in the year 1690 the body of the church, and also the tower, were cased with bricks of an admirable quality, and mortar suitable to them, for at this time there is scarcely any symptoms of decay.

It seems that at one time it underwent some repairs and Pye tells us:

> Some years back, the church of St Martin being under repair, the workmen discovered that the four pinnacles, (one at each corner of the tower), were very much decayed, upon which, the powers at that time in authority concluded, that they should be re-constructed, and to make a finish, fixed a vane upon each of them, without considering, that, the steeple being in the centre, it was not possible for the wind invariably to act upon all alike.

Of St Philip's Church, Pye tells us that 'the site of the churchyard and parsonage and the bluecoat school was the gift of Elizabeth Phillips, and her son and daughter-in-law, Mr and Mrs William Inge, the ancestors of William Phillips Inge Esq'.

Most of the land churches were built on were given by wealthy landowners. Christ Church was built in 1805 on land given by William Phillips Inge, a descendant of Mr and Mrs Inge. St Bartholomew's was a gift of John Jennens in 1749. St James in Ashted was originally the residence of John

Ash. When he left Birmingham, he sold it to John Brooke, who converted it into a church and it was consecrated in 1810.

St Mary's was built on land given by Mrs Weaman in 1774, and five years later Charles Colmore gave a piece of ground for the building of St Paul's, of which Charles Pye says, 'The ground whereon it stands being a declivity, is not altogether suitable for such a pile of building, but at that time it was the most eligible spot at his disposal.' Nevertheless, the 'pile of building' is still standing today.

There were many other denominations in Birmingham and all had their churches and chapels. The first Catholic Church was built on Broad Street in 1789 and then another in Shadwell Street. The Society of Friends had a meeting hall in Bull Street and the Methodists had chapels in Cherry Street, Belmont Row, Bradford Street and Oxford Street. At first the Baptists used a house on the High Street and then Mount Zion on Graham Street until a church was built on Cannon Street. These just name a few.

Before the introduction of public cemeteries the dead were buried in the churchyard of their parish church, but as Charles Pye wrote:

> The different cemeteries within the town being crowded with bodies of the deceased, it was considered proper to purchase three acres of land near to the chapel of St Bartholomew, as an additional burial ground; for which £1,600 was paid to the governors of the Free School. This ground is divided into two parts, each of which is enclosed by a brick wall, surmounted by iron palisades, and gates of the same at the entrance, which is secured by locks. It was consecrated on the 6th of July, 1813, by the bishop of the diocese.

But as mentioned in the chapter, 'Researching your Birmingham Roots', many other public cemeteries were established over the following decades.

The Free Grammar School was founded by King Edward VI in 1552 and the Birmingham school became established in the Guild building on New Street. In the 1730s a new building was built on New Street, which was again replaced a hundred years later. Two hundred years after that, in the 1930s, the school moved to Edgbaston, where it still has an excellent reputation.

In the early 1700s, the Rev. William Higgs, the Rector of St Philip's Church, saw a need for poor children to be educated. Thanks to subscriptions, in 1722 a small piece of land by St Philip's Church was leased with the sole purpose of building a school for the less privileged children of Birmingham. Two years later the building was completed and the first pupils – thirty-two boys and twenty girls – began their lessons there on 9 August 1724. Known as the Bluecoat School, it was enlarged a number of times until a new school was built in the 1930s at Harborne Hill House in Edgbaston, where it still stands today.

In 1813 the National School was opened on Pinfold Street. It housed five hundred boys on the lower floor and four hundred girls on the upper floor. However, only children being brought up in the Church of England were allowed to attend. The building was enclosed with a high brick wall, which included two areas where the boys and the girls could take part in recreational pursuits separately.

Sunday Schools were established at the start of the Industrial Revolution to provide the children of working-class families with some sort of education, to teach them to read and write. Children of these families worked themselves during the week, so Sunday was the only day they could attend classes. Originally introduced in Gloucester, as John Langford wrote in 1868, 'Birmingham was, we rejoice to say, very early in following the example.'

It was said that the children were always neatly clothed and many families would donate a penny a week towards the running of the schools. At the beginning the classes were organised by a committee headed by the Rev. C. Curtis and Rev. J. Riland, and in September 1784 twelve schools were opened in various parts of Birmingham. Within a year 1,400 children had been admitted to these schools. The number increased each year, as Langford wrote that, 'the 1,800 children taught in Sunday schools in 1788, have increased to 26,600 in 1867; for whose reception there are 62 schools, and a staff of zealous, voluntary, and unpaid teachers, extending 2,500 in number, who give up Sunday after Sunday to rescue the children of the poor from the slough of ignorance and sin.'

For adults wanting to have an education there was the Birmingham and Midland Institute, which opened in 1854 and was advertised as 'for the intellectual recreation of the operative classes'. It was founded by an Act of Parliament in 1854 and was the idea of Arthur Ryland. Membership fell into three types: honorary members, members paying large annual subscriptions and those paying only small subscriptions. During the second half of the nineteenth century it provided an education in science, literature, art and technical studies for all classes. It stood on the corner of Paradise Street and Edmund Street, but forty years later the building was purchased by the council to make way for a new road. A new building was built on Margaret Street and the Institute has remained there ever since.

The amenities available included reading rooms and baths, while later a coffee house was added. However, it didn't attract the working classes,

A quiet spot in Cannon Hill Park in the early 1900s but still a beauty spot for the residents of today. (Author's Collection)

and in fact even the middle classes didn't take a lot of interest at first, but it slowly developed and is still popular today.

The Institute is also home to the Free Library Collection, which was set up by John Lee, a button manufacturer, and was categorised by Joseph Priestley. It was originally held in a building in Union Street before being moved to the Institute in Margaret Street. However, arguments seem to have taken place in the early years regarding the types of religious books the library should contain, the difference of opinions being between Anglican and nonconformists, which resulted in the library committee splitting up.

The first library in Birmingham had been set up by the Rev. William Higgs, the first rector of St Philip's in 1733. It was advertised as a free library for the clergymen of the town and neighbourhood and was housed in the parsonage. When it closed in 1927, three hundred of its books were given to the Birmingham Library and they cover a wide range of material from history to philosophy.

The first lending library opened on 6 September 1865 on Edmund Street and it became so popular it had to be extended. But a fire erupted on 11 January 1879 and only 1,000 books were saved of its collection of 50,000. A second building was built on the same site in 1879 and the library remained here until 1973.

It had been decided in 1938 that new, larger premises were needed as the library and its membership had grown, but because of the war this didn't happen. Eventually, in the 1970s a building was built on the new development around Chamberlain Square. Then, on 3 September 2013, the library moved again to another new building in Centenary Square.

The Museum and Art Gallery opened in 1885 in Congreve Street, but again the working classes and some of the middle class showed no interest. There had been a private art gallery in New Street since 1829, which had been created by the Birmingham Society of Artists, but the Museums Act of 1845 saw an opportunity for a public gallery. However, it wasn't until 1864 that the society opened a public exhibition and then in 1878 Jesse Collings, the Mayor of Birmingham, started subscriptions for a purpose-built gallery.

This eventually occupied part of the Council House building, where it is still to be found today.

Our Birmingham ancestors have amused themselves in many different ways according to their status and the era. For the working classes the men would find their relaxation in ale houses and at cock-fights, bull-baiting and dog-fighting, which took place in local taverns. The upper classes had parties and dances. There were theatres where concerts and plays were performed. Exhibitions took place, anything from musical clocks to clockwork figures, fireworks, giants and learned dogs. And there were gardens and parks they could walk in. By the time of the 1835 edition of William Hutton's *History of Birmingham* there were other pastimes for both the working class and the more wealthy, which included cards, dominoes, bagatelle, ball, marbles and cricket.

Bull-baiting was prohibited in 1773, but with the Act not being passed until 1835 to ban it altogether, there were still those who used it as a means of entertainment. As quoted from John Langford's *A Century in Birmingham Life*:

At Chapel Wake, 1798, some law-defying reprobates started a bull baiting in Snow Hill, but the Loyal Association of Volunteers turned out, and with drums beating and colours flying soon put the rebels to flight, pursuing them as far as Birmingham Heath, where the baiters got a beating, the Loyals returning home with the bull as a trophy.

The exhibitions included visits by Madame Tussaud's, and circuses and menageries. In 1793 there was even a model of the guillotine where life-size models were executed. These examples were primarily used by the working classes but at certain times the middle classes did have a certain curiosity.

Like other towns and cities, the public house in Birmingham was the centre of entertainment and in 1770 there were more than 250 taverns and public houses in Birmingham for the working class man to enjoy. These establishments varied from small, gloomy places in back streets to large brightly lit buildings decorated with ornate, polished brass, the latter probably used by the more upper-class working man. In the late nineteenth century the majority were in a 1½-mile radius of New Street as, although expanding outwards, the town centre was still the hub of social life.

There were many working men's clubs and friendly societies in Birmingham. Some of these, although they met in public houses, condemned drunkenness, gambling and swearing, while others met in the schoolrooms or the vestries of churches and chapels. While many groups were formed in the early 1800s, by the 1830s, with the rise of Chartism, it was wondered if educating the working classes was advisable. Hence it was argued that the lives of the workers of Birmingham had never been better; they had never been housed, fed, clothed or taught as well as they now were.

Sport became a pastime enjoyed by all and bowling was considered a respectable pastime for the gentler classes. *Showell's Dictionary* tells us that there were bowling greens at the Hen & Chickens in the High Street in 1741 and at the Union Tavern in Cherry Street in 1792. Aston Hall and Cannon Hill Park provided greens in later years and many suburban hotels and pleasure gardens also had them.

Tennis, archery and croquet were other activities that our ancestors enjoyed, and Birmingham has always been proud to say that lawn tennis arrived in Birmingham before it went to Wimbledon. Today, what is known as the 'warm-up' to Wimbledon is played at the Edgbaston Priory Club. Major Thomas Henry Gem played racquets at the Bath Racquet's Club but one day decided to have a game in his garden at 8 Ampton Court, Edgbaston. He played with his friend, Augurio Perera, a Spanish merchant, and from that the sport as we know it today was born.

With the banning of cruel sports in 1835, an interest began in the newer sports such as cricket, football and gymnastics. Football clubs had their beginnings in church youth groups. Aston Villa Football Club was formed in 1874 by youths connected to Villa Cross Wesleyan Chapel in Handsworth. Their ground was eventually built on what was the kitchen garden of Aston Hall, owned by Sir Thomas Holte. Birmingham City (originally called the Small Heath Alliance) was formed in 1875 by members of the Holy Trinity club. Originally they played in Muntz Street before moving in 1905 to their present ground, St Andrew's, in Bordesley.

The first cricket match recorded was on 15 July 1751 in Apollo Gardens, Deritend, but it was many years before Warwickshire Cricket Club was formed in 1882. Following this, the Birmingham and District Cricket League was introduced in 1888. The Edgbaston Cricket Ground was originally a meadow of grazing land on the Calthorpe estate and the first match was played here against Marylebone CC on 7 June 1886 in front of 3,000 people. Two days later a crowd of 6,000 watched Australia play a two-day match.

Rugby has been played at the ground in Reddings Road, Moseley, since 1873.

Because of its central position and elevation, Birmingham was considered, at one time, to be one of the healthiest in the kingdom. As Showell states in the *Dictionary of Birmingham*, 'Dr Priestley said the air breathed here was as pure as any he had analysed. Were he alive now and in the habit of visiting the neighbourhood of some of our rolling mills &c., it is possible he might return a different verdict.' One can imagine the idle rich strolling and taking in this fresh air of Priestley's day.

Described by Charles Pye as 'the fashionable resort in Birmingham', Vauxhall Gardens in Aston contained a large lawn and was surrounded by a line of trees and small flower beds. In the centre there was a fountain from which pathways went off in all directions. Originally there had been some fine lead statues in the days when they were private gardens owned by the Holte family but, when they were opened to the public some went missing, and so the others were removed. In his, *Description of Modern Birmingham*, Pye wrote:

These delightful gardens, which contain a very spacious bowling green, an orchestra, a great number of commodious gravel walks, on the borders of which are numerous lofty trees, of various kinds, together with parterres, where flowers of different sorts were accustomed to be seen, were, till of late years, resorted to by none but the genteeler sort of people, and their retired situation, are every way capable of being made one of the most rural retreats for public amusement of any in the kingdom.

But at the time of Pye writing his description the ambiance was changing. An alehouse had been erected 'where persons of all descriptions may be accommodated with that or any liquor, on which account the upper classes of the inhabitants have entirely absented themselves'.

Vauxhall Gardens belonged to the Duddeston Hall estate and the first mention of them being opened to the public was an advert in *Aris's Birmingham Gazette* in 1751 regarding the leasing of the property, 'It lies within half a mile of Birmingham and greatly resorted to by the inhabitants thereof, as well as from other places, being used in the publick way, and in the summer season is a concert every other week.'

The gardens were closed in September 1850, when the estate was sold by the daughter of the last male member of the Holte family in order to pay off her husband's debts.

A rival to Vauxhall Gardens, although smaller, were the Apollo Gardens in Deritend. They belonged to Holte Bridgman and although it's not known exactly when he opened them, the first known mention of them was in May 1748 when it was reported that a music concert and fireworks display was to be cancelled due to bad weather. However, in 1751, probably because they didn't prove a financial success, they were closed. Some years later, in 1786, a hotel and gardens were built by the River Rea on the newly built Moseley Street in Deritend. Given the name the Apollo Hotel and Gardens, it also offered concerts, a bowling green and pleasure boat trips. It was very popular for some time but closed in the 1800s, probably due to alterations to the area and the river, and the hotel building was turned into residential properties.

In 1829 the Botanical Gardens were established and White's *Directory* describes it in detail:

The gardens occupy an area of 14 acres, most delightfully situated, having a gentle declivity to the south-west. On entering the Lodge, The

Terrace Walk commands a most beautiful and diversified view, scattered villas, Edgbaston Park, the delightful village of Harborne, the Worcester Canal, and the Birmingham and Gloucester railway, present themselves, with King's Norton Church, in the distance. On the north side, is the magnificent Eliptical Conservatory, one of the most ornamental in the kingdom; the right wing of which is the Green House, and the left a stove for the warmer plants: near to these, are four other Green Houses, for the cultivation of plants. South of the Terrace is the Lawn, which, from the beauty of its undulations, has admitted of the walks being so arranged from which many interesting features are seen; such as the Arboretum, Herbaceous arrangement, Rosarium, Pinetum, and many others. The collection of hardy plants is remarkably good, so are the Stove and Green House collections. In Ferns, the gardens are peculiarly rich.

Our ancestors must have thoroughly enjoyed their walks here, relaxing in the sunshine and taking in the sights. White's *Directory* tells that the shareholders and subscribers to the company had the rights to free admission for themselves and their family of no more than four people, with the general public being charged 1*s* per person and 6*d* for a child under 10. So would our poorer ancestors have been able to enjoy this place of interest? It seems so, as the directory goes on to say, 'The gardens are open on Mondays to the working classes, at the nominal charge of one penny, and great numbers avail themselves of this privilege.'

Other parks and gardens began to appear. Calthorpe Park on Pershore Road was given to the town by Lord Calthorpe in 1857 and became the first public park in Birmingham. Later, in 1873 Miss Ryland, gave the land that became Cannon Hill Park.

For children, the first park was developed in 1854 by Joseph Sturge, who as *Showell's* relates, 'set apart a field in Wheeley's Lane as a public playground for children, and this must rank as the first recreation ground'.

By the time of White's *Directory* of 1849, swimming was becoming a popular pastime, although there had been an interest in bathing for a number of centuries. However, with the arrival of the railways people were venturing further afield and were discovering the benefits of swimming in the sea. Parliament decided to encourage local authorities to provide some kind of swimming and wash house facilities in the larger towns and the Baths and Washhouses Act was passed in 1846.

Birmingham already had baths in Ladywell, somewhere near Hurst Street, which were supplied with water from the nearby springs. According to White's *Directory* of 1849, they contained a suite of nineteen baths. The ladies' bath was made of marble and all suites had a private dressing room. The swimming pool was 100ft long and 50ft wide with a depth rising from 3ft to 5. There were separate boxes fronting the water and a dressing room.

After the 1846 Act, another baths was built in George Street, Balsall Heath, and was described by White's *Directory* as being 'situated in the most salubrious air round Birmingham and to have a continual supply of pure water, and the surrounding scenery most beautiful'.

Theatrical performances have always been something enjoyed by all classes of people. In the early centuries strolling players travelled the country, setting up their booths and providing entertainment wherever they could. However, in Birmingham in 1730 a very basic building, similar to a stable, was erected in Castle Street for the use of strolling players. Ten years later the first theatre, the New Theatre, was built in Moor Street, and then during the 1740s two more were built, one in New Street and the other in Smallbrook Street. Unfortunately these were both short-lived and by 1751 had disappeared. The following year, a theatre opened in King Street, but that same year the theatre in Moor Street closed and was converted into a Methodist chapel. However, this proved unpopular with some of the population and when the congregation left after a service held by Wesley they were stoned by a mob.

It was in 1774 that theatre life really took off with the building of the Theatre Royal in New Street. An extra colonnade was added in 1780 and Charles Pye described it as, 'one of the most elegant theatres in Europe'. After a fire in 1792 the proprietors purchased adjoining buildings and over the next four years the theatre was enlarged. However, due to it being in line with the rest of the buildings on New Street it was difficult to appreciate it. In 1807 it was renamed the Royal Theatre.

The Prince of Wales Theatre, initially known as the Royal Music Hall Operetta House, opened in Broad Street in 1856. Containing an impressive organ, it provided what was described as 'high-class concerts'. Other theatres appeared in the 1860s, but they didn't last long. These were the New Theatre in Moor Street and the Empire Theatre, also known as Day's Music Hall, on the corner of Hurst Street and Smallbrook Street. Both gave the public a varied choice of entertainment. In the 1880s and '90s the Grand Theatre, the Queen's Theatre and the Imperial Theatre opened but again were short-lived. Then in 1899 the Hippodrome opened and, in 1901, the Alexandra. Both are still open today.

The Birmingham Repertory Theatre opened in February 1913 with a production of *Twelfth Night*. Its manager, Barry Jackson, saw it as a place to provide a platform for both new plays and the revival of old ones, and his enthusiasm paid off with the New Repertory Theatre on Broad Street still providing that platform. Many of our older generation of great actors started their careers in the small Station Street theatre, including Lawrence Olivier and Ralph Richardson.

Some of our ancestors may have been professional actors and appeared in these theatres, but they may also have been thespians in ways some people are today, as amateur theatre was as popular as it is today.

The Birmingham Amateur Dramatic Association was formed in 1856 at an annual subscription of one guinea. By 1900 there were many successful 'am dram' societies all over Birmingham; some specific to an area, others with a local church or school.

If you find or think you had an ancestor in either the professional or amateur theatre, a search in the newspaper index will hopefully give you a glimpse into their acting life.

The early 1900s brought new entertainment, the cinema. In 1915 Curzon Hall, originally built in 1864, became the West End Cinema and could accommodate an audience of 3,000. The proprietor, Walter Jeffs, had already been including the showing of films in his productions, which were, as noted in the *Birmingham Daily Mail*, 'now established as one of the recreation institutions of the city, and the fact that they never fail to attract large audiences is due to their artistic merit'. Cinemas continued to 'attract large audiences' and by 1930 there were eighty-three in Birmingham, entertaining 80,000 customers.

As the *Victoria County History's* edition in 1964 tells us, 'they were all shapes and sizes, raging from central "super-cinemas" with neon lights, thick carpets, and expensive foyers to old picture palaces, still surviving, as some of the old inns survived in an age of great suburban public houses, as monuments to a not very distant past.'

Visiting restaurants doesn't seem to be something our ancestors did, as *Showell's* reports, 'Our grandfathers knew them not. They took their chop or steak at their inn or hotel, or visited the tripe houses. Indeed Joe Allday's tripe shop in Union Street (opened about 1839–40) may be called the "restaurant" established here, as it was the favourite resort of many Town Councillors and leading men of the town.' In 1881 a vegetarian restaurant opened on Paradise Street and in 1883 a fish restaurant opened in Warwick Passage, which was described as 'a novelty'.

However, dining with friends seems to have been quite an experience on some occasions, as Thomas Anderton relates. He was born in 1836, so one can assume this example may have taken place in the late 1850s, perhaps 1860s:

In my younger days my host would invite members of his family and some friends to dinner at two o'clock. The dinner proper – which was a good, substantial, and even luxurious meal – being over, we adjourned to the drawing room. There the desert would be laid out on a large round table around which we gathered. Then mine host would call for his wine book – for he had a well-stocked cellar of fine vintages. Turning over the leaves of this book he would propose to begin with a bottle of '47 port which was then a comparatively young and fruity wine. This would be followed probably by a bottle of 1840, and then we should come to the great 1834 wine, of which mine host had a rare stock.

Sometimes we should hark back to 1820 port, a wine which I remember to have had a rich colour and a full refined flavour, and once I tasted the famous comet wine, 1811, which, however, had lost something of its nucleus, and only retained a certain tawny, nebulous tone. On one occasion I remember my host said he had some seventeen-ninety something wine in this cellar, which he proposed we should taste, but for some reason, now forgotten, it was not produced, and I sometimes rather regret that I so narrowly missed the opportunity of tasting a last century wine. Perhaps it may be thought from the procession of ports produced on such occasions as I have described that we indulged in a sustained and wine-bibbing bout. But it was not so. In reality we only just tasted each vintage, so that we had the maximum of variety with the minimum of quantity.

The wine ended, we betook ourselves into another room, there to enjoy a cigar. Then would come tea and coffee, and a little music. Supper – yes, my reader, a good supper would be announced about nine o'clock; after that another little smoke, and about ten o'clock or soon after we should take our departure.

I also remember once being at an unfrugal, festive dinner at a friend's house, when one of the guests proposed our host's health, and finished up by saying, 'I shall be glad to see everyone at this table to dinner at my house this day week.' Considering there were about thirty persons sitting round the mahogany this was a fair-sized order. But it was no empty compliment. The dinner came off, and a fine good spread it was, and as for the wine I seem to sniff its bouquet now.

Some of the old Birmingham men whose characteristic hospitalities I have just described had certain habits which, looked at by modern light, would seem somewhat plebeian. For instance, there were men of wealth and importance who made it their custom often to go and spend an hour or two in the evening at some of the old respectable hotels and inns of the town. They had been in the habit of meeting together at these hostelries in their earlier days to talk over the news, at a period when daily local newspapers were not published, and they adhered to the custom in their advanced years, and rejoiced in visiting their old haunts and smoking their long clay pipes, and having a chat with old friends and kindred spirits.

All this has died out now. For one thing, most of these old inns and hostelries have disappeared with the march of modern times. We have clubs now and restaurants, also hotels where visitors put-up, but the old fashioned inns and taverns have mostly gone.

The twentieth century brought troubles that the people of Birmingham had never known. The First World War took the lives of many young men, and some left wives behind with young children who were never to meet their fathers. Men came home scarred by not only the physical wounds they had received but mental ones, too. Whole families were affected and sons and brothers were lost. And the general feeling of those of younger generations who talked about their family's loss years later was 'and apparently it was never talked about'.

Twenty-one years later those families were to suffer again in a war that this time came right up to their doorsteps. Couples and families who survived the previous war could suddenly, without hardly any warning, be wiped out by Hitler's bombs. Children were separated from their mothers. Peter Jones

Aston Hall, Birmingham.

Aston Hall. Built in the early 1600s for Sir Thomas Holte, the Jacobean mansion was also home to James Watt junior between 1817 and 1848. (Author's Collection)

tells that his father, David, and his uncle were evacuated to Gloucester in September 1939:

> however they returned to Nechells in summer 1940, after which the blitz kicked off and in autumn '40 they were evacuated to Barton under Needwood. Dad and his older brother were looked after firstly by a well-to-do family who had a maid so they were well fed and bathed. He enjoyed school but when the maid was called up for the war effort they were moved to a less grand home where there was a well, and outside loo. That was the end of daily baths. Nonetheless Dad loved it there.

Anderson air-raid shelters were issued. Made of six corrugated iron curved sheets, they were joined together with bolts. One end was covered and the other left open as the entrance. They were erected in the back yard and families would sleep in them all night, every night. They were supposedly safer and, of course, more private than public shelters. They could still hear the noise and every morning left their shelters wondering what sights they were going to see.

Those who couldn't enlist in the armed forces joined the Home Guard. Ivor Roth tells us that his father, Ernest, and his nephew, Maurice, were on home guard duty at Holloway Head:

> their duty was to shovel sand over any fires to make the targets not visible to the German bombers. Suddenly there was a huge explosion and the whole rear wall of a building vanished. When the ash dust had gone, they saw on the fourth floor a bed visible from the street. They climbed the stairs to investigate if anyone was in the building. They found an elderly lady still in bed. Of course her outside wall had gone and if she exited the bed to her right she would have had a nasty awakening. My dad said they gingerly went over to her and woke her up. They said you need to get out of bed but don't get out the other side. She was deaf and had not heard the din of the bomb.

Birmingham wasn't despondent and after many years was eventually built up again. New roads, new houses and high-rise flats appeared, and one wonders what Hutton, Pye, Anderton and others would have said.

7

Around Birmingham
and its Suburbs

Birmingham has seen many changes, and not just with its trade and its people but its surroundings, too. So let us take a walk along some of the streets as described many years ago by other historians.

Showell's *Dictionary of Birmingham* tells us that Edgbaston Street is:

> one of the most ancient streets in the Borough, having been the original road from the parish church and the Manor-house of the Lords de Bermingham to their neighbours at Edgbaston. It was the first paved street of the town, and the chosen residence of the principal and most wealthy.

Known in King John's reign as 'Egebaston Strete', it was most certainly paved at that time as the word 'strete' described a paved way in towns and cities. At one time there were several tanneries at the bottom of Edgbaston Street as a stream ran from the moat around Parsonage House to the Manor House, 'the watercourse being now known as Dean Street and Smithfield Passage'. Here too was the Lady Well, a spring that was never known to fail and therefore dedicated to the Virgin Mary. The stream from it provided water for the moat around the Parsonage and then it continued at the back of Edgbaston Street, by Smithfield Passage and Dean Street, to the Manor House moat.

'Rivalling Edgbaston Street in its antiquary' is Moor Street. Its origin is not really known but is thought to have been where a mill existed in the fourteenth century. The miller was John le Moul and it is thought that the name derived from this. However from its earliest date it was the chosen place of residence for many of the old Birmingham families such as Carless, Smalbroke, Ward, Sheldon, Flavell and Stidman.

Some of the roads leading into and out of Birmingham in the olden days were little better than deep ruts, which were more or less levelled about the middle of last century. The making of the great Holyhead coach-road also graded some of the steeper spots as well as the lowest, but the modern town improvements must be credited as the greatest factor in the levelling of the roads, none of which, however, were 'macadamised' until 1818.

In his book *Modern Birmingham* of 1818, Charles Pye described some of the walks he took around the town. It is difficult to imagine the area around Birmingham commanding wonderful views, so perhaps it is best left to his words. One such journey was taken in the direction of Bromsgrove:

You proceed up Smallbrook-street, when a spacious road opens to the left, and being clear of the buildings, the spire of King's Norton church, which is six miles distant, forms a pleasing object. On the left you have a picturesque view of the country, which continues without any intermission nearly the space of three miles. There is in this valley, what is very unusual to be seen in such a situation, a windmill; and as you proceed, there are in the same valley several water mills, that are made use of by the Birmingham manufacturers. This view is skirted by buildings erected on the road to Alcester and when you near the two mile stone, you perceive among the trees, Moseley Hall, which is a modern stone building; the residence of Mrs Taylor. Exactly, opposite, on the right hand, is the parish church of Edgbaston, and also the hall, which is surrounded by a park, wherein are some lofty trees, and an extensive sheet of water. This mansion house, or hall, is now occupied by Edward Johnson, M.D. a person of considerable eminence in his profession.

A short distance beyond the three mile stone the road crosses the Worcester canal; from which bridge, if you look towards Birmingham, there is a rich and variegated landscape, consisting of hill, dale, wood, and water.

The 1841 census shows that Edward Johnson, physician, is still living at Edgbaston Hall. There were other descriptive walks:

You proceed down Snowhill, and having passed the one mile stone, there are a few trees close to the road side, and opposite to them there is an extensive view over Barr-beacon, and the adjacent country, including the lofty trees in Aston park, over whose tops, the elegant spire of that church is seen. In descending the hill, when you have passed the buildings, the eye is delighted, on the right hand, with an extensive view over Hunter's nursery grounds, and on the left is Hockley abbey: this building was erected upon a piece of waste, boggy land, about 1779, by Mr. Richard Ford, an engenius mechanic of Birmingham, who, among other things invented a one-wheel carriage, which he constructed entirely of iron. You now cross the Bourn, a small stream of water, that separates Warwickshire from the county of Stafford, and passes by Mr Boulton's plantations on the left, when you are about half way up the hill, there is on the right hand, Prospect-house, where the late Mr. Eginton carried on his manufactory of stained glass. At the two mile stone, on the left, is the entrance to Soho, where Matthew Robinson Boulton, Esq. resides, who is proprietor of the Soho Manufactory.

Another journey took him in a different direction to the Soho area:

Having passed the Sand-pits and Spring-hill, you cross the Birmingham canal and enter upon what was Birmingham-heath, which being enclosed in the year 1800, was found to contain 289 acres, which land now lets from thirty to fifty shillings per acre. On the right hand is a boat-builders yard, and on the left a glass-house, belonging to Messrs. Biddle and Lloyds. Proceeding towards the windmill, you perceive at a short distance on the right hand another glass-house, belonging to Messrs Shakespear and Fletcher. Ascending the hill, there is on the right an extensive view over the adjacent country, including Barr-beacon, Mr Boulton's plantations, and Winson-green, a neat house, in the possession of Mrs Steward. On the left is Summerfield-house, late residence of John Iddins, Esq. but now of James Woolley, Esq. and beyond it, a neat white house, occupied by Mr Hammon.

If we take the wards and parliamentary constituencies that now belong to the Birmingham City Council, we find very little to the west of the city centre, apart from Handsworth in the north-west and Edgbaston in the south-west. It has been said that Smethwick, to the west, fought many times to remain separate from the Birmingham district and on one occasion won by just one vote. The furthest north is Sutton Coldfield. To the south, Northfield, King's Norton and Selly Oak and in the east Castle Bromwich, Sheldon and Yardley. At one time these belonged to the counties of either Worcestershire or Warwickshire but after various extension acts, where Birmingham's boundaries were changed, they gradually became part of the Birmingham district.

So let us take a look at the history of some of these places and their neighbours.

Aston

Aston was an extensive parish and at one time seems to have dwarfed the neighbouring market town of Birmingham. In fact, according to St Peter and St Paul's, the parish church, the Domesday Book values Aston at 100s, whereas Birmingham, only 20s. However, Wright's *Directory* in 1849 gives

Blakesley Hall, renovated and back to how it was in its glory days. (Author's Photograph)

a slightly different view: 'by the Domesday survey, it is called eight hides, valued at £5. Per annum, a mill 3s; and a wood three miles long, and half-a-mile broad'. William Hutton tells us that up until the mid-1700s there were more baptisms, marriages and burials in Aston parish than that of Birmingham parish. White's *Directory* also describes it as 'an extensive, well-built, scattered village occupying a descent to the River Tame; containing in its hamlet 943 acres'.

Aston Hall was occupied by the Holte family but when Sir Charles Holte died in 1782 there was no male heir, so the property passed to his daughter, Mary. Mary was the wife of Abraham Bracebridge, who had fallen into some financial difficulty and so the estate was sold. The hall at one time was owned by the Watt family, but the gardens and park were acquired by the Birmingham Corporation, who opened them as a public park. At a later date the hall was turned into a museum and art gallery.

Charles Pye's excursions took him through Aston on his way to Sutton Coldfield:

You leave Birmingham, through Aston-street and the adjacent buildings in the parish of Aston, which extend for a considerable distance along the road. Having passed the buildings, you soon after cross a small stream of water that has performed its office of turning a corn mill, which you perceive on your left hand. This mill was within memory a forge, for the making of bar iron – there is another mill upon the same stream, a short distance above, known by the name of Aston furnace, which was a blast furnace for the purpose of making pig iron to supply the forge below. This mill has been considerably enlarged, and a steam engine erected contiguous to it, and is now used as a paper mill. From an adjacent hill there is a good view over the town of Birmingham.

A lofty brick wall now presents itself to view, by which the park belonging to Aston hall is surrounded: it being by computation three miles in circumference; within which there is a great abundance of valuable timber, and it is also well stocked with deer. When the wall recedes from the high road, keep by the side of it, which leads you to the parish church, and also to the mansion house or hall, which is a brick building, erected by Sir Thomas Holt, at the same time that he enclosed the park. The hall has of late years been in possession of Heneage Legge, Esq. but is at present unoccupied, and the whole estate is upon sale. (Since writing the above, the mansion of Aston, together with the park, had been purchased by Messrs. Greenway and Whitehead, of Warwick, who have converted the house into two tenements, disposed of the deer, turned the park into enclosures, and fallen the timber.)

The church dedicated to St Peter and St Paul, is a stone building, with a lofty spire, and contains several monuments of the Holt family; it is also ornamented with two windows of stained glass, by Eginton.

Sir Lister Holt, the late proprietor of this estate, not having children, and being at variance with his only brother, (who succeeded to the title), he entailed the estate upon four different families, none of whom had or

Sarehole Mill, tucked away on the edge of parkland in Hall Green. (Author's Photograph)

are likely to have any children, although they have been in possession of it for the space of near forty years.

Ashted, a suburb in Aston, took its name from Dr John Ash, a wealthy surgeon and one of the founders of the General Hospital. In 1771 he leased land from Sir Lister Holte, which, after he moved to London, was sold to John Brooke. He developed the land building houses for the rich who had made their money in the new industries in Birmingham and wanted to move to the country. John Ash's house, which he had built for himself, was converted into the parish church of St James the Less. Badly damaged by German bombs, it was demolished in 1956.

Overlooking Vauxhall Gardens is Duddeston Hall, which also belonged to the Holte family. The first record of this family seems to be in 1331 when Simon del Holte bought the manor of Nechells, and then in 1365 when John Holte bought the manor of Duddeston, where his descendants lived for many centuries. Being part of Aston parish, the church here has many effigies and memorials in honour of the family, the earliest being that of William Holte, who died in September 1514. Sir Thomas Holte began the building of Aston Hall in 1618 and eventually moved there in 1631. Charles I visited in October 1642 but the following year it was visited by the Parliamentarians, who held the hall for three days. Sir Thomas was imprisoned and the hall plundered.

Saltley

Further east is Saltley and it was on the Washwood Heath Road that William Hutton lived, which Charles Pye passed on one of his excursions:

> You now pass through the village of Saltely, and at the extremity, on the left, is Bennett's Hill, where Mr William Hutton, the venerable historian of Birmingham resided, and ended his days. This residence, so denominated by the proprietor, was originally a very small house, with the entrance in the centre, and a small room on each side, to which has been added two wings, or rather rooms, being only one story in height: there is a wall by the road side, five feet high, the top of which is on a level with the top of the parlour windows; the entrance of it having been altered from the front to the side. His peculiar manner of writing, his quaint expressions, and the tales he relates of himself, have caused a considerable sale for his productions, and numerous people, when they are taking an excursion, will travel some distance to view the residence of their favourite author.

The estate belonged to the Adderley family, who lived at Saltley Hall before moving to Hams Hall north of Coleshill. The hall has long since gone but the grounds, donated by Charles Adderley in the 1850s, were developed into Adderley Park.

Saltley was once an area of farm land and was the last to be enclosed in Birmingham. The corn grown in the fields was ground in a water mill on the River Rea at Crawford Street. In the 1880s the mill became part of the gas works. White's 1849 *Directory* states that, 'a great number of new houses have been erected during the last four or five years'. This was probably due to the building of a railway carriage works there in 1845 by Joseph Wright, so very soon a small community of working-class properties were built along the High Street and Gate Street.

Saltley belonged to the parish of Aston but Joseph Wright also donated money for the building of a church and St Saviour's Church was consecrated in 1850.

Erdington

Erdington in 1841 had a population of 2,579, contained 442 houses and was described in 1849 by White's *Directory* as a 'considerable well-built village'. It was listed in the Domesday Book as Hardingtone and up until the early 1800s belonged to the parish of Aston. Once very much a rural area, it was the development of the canal system and the railways that led to its expansion. In 1823 the church of St Barnabas was opened as a chapel of ease.

Erdington Hall was built in 1650 on the site of an old medieval hall by John Jennens, the wealthy ironmonger. Following his death in 1651 his son, Humphrey, going one step higher and becoming an iron-maker, erected his furnaces at nearby Bromford. The Jennens family remained at Erdington Hall until the late 1700s but, no doubt due to Erdington's expansion, they moved away to Nether Whitaker and the hall passed through other hands, eventually losing its past glory. It was demolished in 1912 when the Tyburn Road was built.

Perhaps by 1818 the hall was already in decline, as Charles Pye wrote, 'The village of Erdington does not contain any object deserving of attention, but a little beyond on the right is Pipe Hall, an ancient seat of the Bagot family, now occupied by the Rev. Egerton Bagot.'

Pype Hayes Hall was built *c.* 1635 when Hervey Bagot married Dorothy Arden and was given the land as a dowry. It remained in the family until 1906, when it was bought by James Rollason, the wire manufacturer of Bromford Mills.

A public house on Bromford Lane, the Lad in the Lane, was once known as the Old Green Man and argues against the Old Crown in Digbeth that it is the oldest pub in Birmingham. It is known that parts of the building do date back to the fourteenth century.

Sutton Coldfield

According to descriptions in various directories throughout the 1800s, Sutton developed from being a small market town to an extensive parish, corporate town and polling place for the northern division of the county. Still being considered part of Warwickshire, the majority of family history records are kept at Warwick Record Office, although there are some archival bundles held in the Library of Birmingham.

Pye suggests the name was derived from the name South Town, presumably being south of Lichfield, and that by corruption it became known as Sutton. He goes on to say that, 'there is a very considerable portion of land near this town, where travellers say the air is equally sharp and cold as it is upon the highlands of Scotland, and from this circumstance the latter part of its name originates'.

There was a spring here called Rounton Well:

whose water is remarkably cold and produces a very copious stream, to which numerous people who are afflicted with cutaneous disorders resort, and derive considerable benefit from drinking and bathing therein. It cures the most virulent itch in the human species, and also the mange in dogs, if sufficient care is taken to wash them well in the stream, but a slight washing will not produce the desired effect.

St Mary's, the parish church of Selly Oak. (Author's Photograph)

The 1835 Pigot's *Directory* describes Sutton Coldfield as a market town and parish of 'considerable antiquity' that in ancient times was known as Sutton-Colville and also King's Sutton. John Harman, Bishop Vesey of Exeter at the time of Henry VIII, was born here and during his lifetime he rebuilt a large part of the church, known as Holy Trinity, and built a town hall, a market house and a free grammar school. In 1835 it seems there was just one long street with modern houses and, adjacent to this, the large park. *Kelly's Directory* of 1872 refers to these houses being 'of red brick', and that 'within the last few years a great many villas have been erected in the town, and neighbourhood, and the place is fast becoming a residential suburb for Birmingham'. However, 'the inhabitants are chiefly engaged in agriculture'.

Sutton Park was a Royal Forest belonging to the Saxon Kings of Mercia that became a medieval deer park and was then gifted to the people of Sutton by Henry VIII.

Castle Bromwich

To the east is Castle Bromwich, which was an area of farms and countryside but was described in the 1820s as being a busy and bustling town on market days. White's 1849 *Directory* described it as 'an extensive hamlet, chapelry, and scattered village containing 2,702 acres of land, and, in 1841, 132 houses and 779 inhabitants'.

Bromwich Hall, described by *White's* as 'an ancient brick mansion [which] is the property of the Earl of Bradford, who occasionally resides here'. It was built during the reign of Elizabeth I by Edward Devereux, 1st Baronet of Castle Bromwich, and bought in 1657 by Orlando Bridgeman. The Bridgemans later became the Earls of Bradford, and the hall remained in the family until 1936. It is now a hotel but the gardens are open to the public.

It was to Castle Bromwich that William Hutton escaped during the riots of 1791. He stayed at the Bridgeman Arms on the Chester Road.

Again, family history records are split between Warwick Record Office and the Library of Birmingham, so always check their websites and indexes before visiting either of these places.

Yardley

In the 1800s Yardley was a large parish, which also included Stetchford and Hall Green, belonging to Worcestershire. The church, St Edburgha's, dates back to the thirteenth century. The *Directory & Gazetteer of the County of Worcester*, published in 1855, describes Yardley as:

> a very extensive parish, about 4 miles from Birmingham. The soil is fruitful, and the neighbourhood exceedingly pleasant, abounding with numerous gentlemen's seats and villas. It is divided from Warwickshire by the river Cole, over which are several bridges. The parish contained according to the last census, 2753 inhabitants.

Bournville Carillon was a gift from George Cadbury to his workers after seeing the Bruges carillon in Belgium. (Author's Photograph)

Selly Manor. Another building given to Bournville by George Cadbury.
(Author's Photograph)

Pye tells us that 'the land in this parish being very suitable for making tiles, innumerable quantities are there manufactured, for the supply of Birmingham'.

Blakesley Hall was built in 1590 by Richard Smallbroke as a farmhouse. The Smallbrokes (also known as Smallbrook) were wealthy landowners and it is a descendant of Richard, another Richard, who became the Bishop of Lichfield and Coventry, that the now busy Smallbrook Queensway is named after. In 1685 the hall was sold to the Rev. Dr Henry Greswolde, Rector of Solihull, and for 200 years it was occupied by various tenant farmers. In 1899 it had become dilapidated and was bought by Henry Donne, who renovated it and sold it to Thomas Merry, a paint and varnishing manufacturer. It is now a museum.

During the 1800s rich industrialists, wanting to move to the countryside from the now expanding Birmingham, came here. Soon building work

The Old Grammar School in Kings Norton, winner of BBC's *Restoration* and now preserved for future generations to enjoy. (Author's Photograph)

began and new houses and streets spread all over the parish. Later, in the 1870s, others were attracted here. At this time the Albert Road estate was built, which was aimed at alluring the middle-class commuters as Stetchford railway station was only a five-minute walk away. The population now quickly increased. In 1861 the population was 3,000 and in 1891 it had risen to 17,000. By 1907 there was a population of 58,000 with 13,640 houses.

Originally belonging to Worcestershire, family history records for Yardley are split between The Hive in Worcester and the Library of Birmingham. So again check where the record you want to search is held.

Sheldon

Sheldon was a small village with a small community scattered around the countryside. In 1821 it had a population of 423 and a hundred years later that had only risen to 446. In 1931 it had now increased by 80 people. It was not until the 1930s that Sheldon started to develop, which was a lot later than other places. Large housing estates were built here and now it became a sprawling residential area.

The settlement was originally known as Machitone (Macca's farm) and through many centuries there was a large farm here known as Mackadown. This is now immortalised by the road running through known as Mackadown Lane.

Acocks Green

Acocks Green was just a village right up until the mid-1800s but by 1885 was said, according to *Showell's Dictionary*, to be 'fast becoming a thriving suburban town'.

Named after the Acock family, who built a large house on the Warwick road called Acock's Green House in the fourteenth century, possibly around 1370, it remained a small settlement until the coming of the railways. Acocks Green station was built in 1852 and, like its neighbours, the village now became a desirable place to live for the wealthier workers and tradespeople of Birmingham. The first part to be developed was Sherbourne Road. In 1881 the population numbered about 10,000, rising to 60,000 by 1911.

Up until the 1860s, Acocks Green belonged to the parish of Yardley but in 1866 St Mary's Church was consecrated and became the parish church for Acocks Green.

Five Ways as it once was. It is now a large and busy traffic island servicing five busy roads. (Author's Collection)

Hall Green

There was a water mill here by the River Cole from very early times, with the original building replaced in 1542. Known as Biddles Mill, it later became known as High Wheel Mill and between 1756 and 1761 was leased by Matthew Boulton, who used it to produce sheet metal for the button industry. In 1771 it was again rebuilt and remained in use until 1919. Now known as Sarehole Mill, it has been renovated into a museum.

The mill's claim to fame is that J.R.R. Tolkien lived close by and said that the mill and area inspired him when writing his books set in Middle Earth.

Charles Pye visited Hall Green on one of his journeys and the following piece takes in one or two other places that have already been written about:

You proceed through Deritend, up Camp Hill, and when near the summit, there is on the right hand an ancient brick building, called the Ravenhurst, the residence of Mr John Lowe, attorney, who is equally

St Bartholomew's, the parish church of Edgbaston, also known as Edgbaston Old Church. There was a chapel here from the fourteenth century, when Edgbaston belonged to the Harborne parish. (Author's Photograph)

respectable in his profession, as the house is in appearance. A short distance beyond on the left is Fair-hill, where Samuel Lloyd, Esq. resides, and on the opposite side of the road is the Larches, the abode of Wm. Withering, Esq. – This house, when it belonged to Mr Darbyshire, was known by the name of Foul Lake, but when Dr. Priestley resided there, he gave it the name of Fair-hill; afterwards, being purchased by Dr. Withering, he altered the name of it to the Larches. Having passed through the turnpike, on the left is Sparkbrook-house, John Rotton, Esq. resident. At the distance of one mile and a half the road to Warwick branches off to the left, and on the summit of the hill is Spark-hill-house, inhabited by Miss Morris. Opposite the three mile stone is a very neat pile of building, called Green-bank-house, where Benjamin Cooke, Esq. has taken up his abode. A little beyond, at a place called the Coal-bank, there is a free school, which is

Winterbourne House was built in 1903 for John Nettlefold, and matches Anderton's description of houses in Edgbaston. Winterbourne is now a museum. (Author's Photograph)

endowed with about forty pounds per annum. At a short distance on the left is Marston chapel, which is usually called Hall-green chapel: it was erected and endowed by Job Marston, Esq. of Hall-green Hall, with about 90 acres of land, and other donations.

At the distance of five miles, you pass through a village called Shirley Street; and at a distance of another five miles, you arrive at Hockley-house; a place of entertainment, where travellers of every denomination are accommodated in a genteel manner, and on reasonable terms.

Balsall Heath

In ancient times Balsall Heath was known as Boswell Heath, and up until 1852 belonged to the King's Norton parish.

Another area of farmland, it was situated on the Moseley Road overlooking the Rea valley, and again the 1830s saw the start of development with new houses and roads being built. The first were on land owned by the Rev. Vincent Edward. Known as the Edwards Estate, they encompassed the new streets of Edward Street (now known as Edward Road), Mary Street, George Street and Tindal Street. Once again, the villa-type houses were built to attract the middle classes of Birmingham.

With the growth of the area St Paul's Church was built in 1853, but by the 1970s it was in need of repair and the struggling congregation were unable to keep it going. They joined forces with the United Reformed Church and the new Balsall Heath Church Centre was built. The old church has now been demolished.

Moseley

Like its neighbour Balsall Heath, Moseley originally belonged to the parish of King's Norton, although the chapelry of Moseley dates back to the early fifteenth century. Moseley started as a Saxon settlement but by the late 1800s was a fashionable Victorian suburb. In 1851 the population was 1500 but by 1911 it had risen to 17,000.

With a change in parish borders in 1853 the chapel became the parish church for Moseley and St Mary's underwent renovation.

Moseley Hall was built in 1632 by the Greaves family, who were wealthy local landowners. It was later bought by John Taylor. Following the damage it received in the 1791 riots it was rebuilt in 1796. Bought by Richard Cadbury in 1884, he donated it to the people in 1892 and it became a children's convalescent home.

Pye mentioned the hall in one of his walks:

you leave Birmingham, either through Alcester-street or up Camphill, where there is a half-timbered house, inhabited by Mr John Simcox, an attorney. In a field nearly opposite there is perhaps the best view over the town of Birmingham that can be taken. In a field near the two mile stone, there is a grand panoramic view of Birmingham, and the adjacent country for several miles on each side of it, which is seen to the greatest advantage in an afternoon. A little beyond is Moseley Hall, an elegant stone building, erected about twenty-five years since, by the late John Taylor, Esq. and is now the residence of his widow.

With so much development taking place, it was a concern that the grounds of Moseley Hall would be developed. However, they weren't. But by 1890 building work was taking place all over the suburbs of Birmingham and this did include the parish of Moseley as new houses slowly spread down the Alcester Road from Balsall Heath.

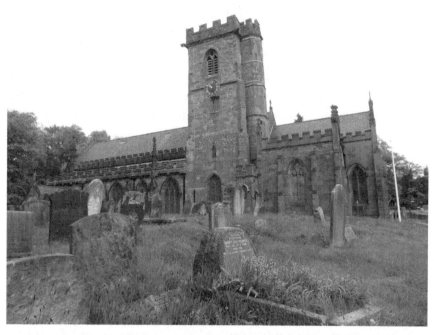

St Mary's, the parish church of Handsworth. First consecrated in the twelfth century, this present church dates back to 1820. It is also known as Handsworth Old Church. (Author's Photograph)

Kings Heath

A sparse area of land in the King's Norton parish enclosure took place in 1774 as part of the enclosure award for the King's Norton parish but it wasn't until the 1870s that Kings Heath began to grow. In fact, between the census of 1871 and 1881 the population grew by a thousand, with predictions that it was likely to double in the next ten years.

Once an uninhabited heath, Kings Heath had begun to develop in a small way during the 1700s after the road between Birmingham and Alcester was improved. Previously it was just a track across the heath that gave farmers from as far afield as Evesham access to the Birmingham markets. Now more accessible, a small village of farms and homesteads soon sprang up along this road.

The first inn along this road was the Cross Guns, which was created from two cottages that already stood there. A pear tree was planted around the same time (*c.* 1774) and because of this the pub eventually became known as The Pear Tree. A brewery behind the inn was built in 1831.

A railway station opened in 1840, so once again a small village on the outskirts of Birmingham started to grow, although some of Birmingham's wealthy residents had already built elaborate homes in Kings Heath in the 1700s. Brass founder William Hamper built The Grange and John Cartland, also a brass founder, built The Priory.

Selly Oak

Selly Oak's history goes back many years mainly due to its close proximity to the Roman camp at Metchley. At first it was just a small manor in the parish of Northfield but it came into its own when the canal reached it in 1792. Sturge's phosphorous factory arrived first, followed by Elliotts Metal Company. Large industries needed workers and workers needed homes, and so Selly Oak took shape.

The name Selly Oak has been the topic of many stories. Scylf Leah, its ancient name, meaning shelf meadow, describes a 'clearing on a shelf of land' and would be typically Saxon. It would also fit with the area having been in the Forest of Arden. Another name was Salt-ley, a meadow in which salt wagons traversed.

Another story tells of the famous oak tree of Selly Oak and refers to the name being a derivative of Sally's Oak where a local witch was buried with an oak stake through her heart that later grew into an oak tree. A mythical tale but the tree did exist, although when it was planted is debatable. Some say it was planted by John Rodway to commemorate the coronation of William VI but the name Selly Oak had already appeared on canal plans sometime before then.

It did grow in the grounds of Selly Oak House though, which stood on the corner of Oak Tree Lane and Bristol Road. Unfortunately, with the expansion that took place in the late 1800s, building work damaged its roots and it became what is known as a stag-oak. Consequently, in May 1909, it was chopped down. The stump was placed in Selly Oak Park with a brass plaque saying, 'Butt of Old Oak Tree from which the name Selly Oak was derived. Removed from Oak Tree Lane, Selly Oak, 1909.' Some years later the old stump underwent dendrochronology (tree dating) tests that suggested it originated from between 1710 and 1730.

Selly Oak belonged to the parish of Northfield until 1862, at which time St Mary's Church was consecrated.

Bournville

Bournville was built by George Cadbury, mainly for his workers to give them a countryside life away from Birmingham. When his factory in the centre of Birmingham had become too small, he went in search of new premises with the idea that an industrial area didn't need to be squalid and gloomy. He found what he was looking for in land between Selly Oak and King's Norton. As it was close to the Bourne Brook he called it Bournville. 'The Factory in the Garden', as it was nicknamed, was built in 1879, the first brick being laid in January and the first chocolate being produced in September.

The area was extended in 1893 to build homes for the workers. These were not the normal back-to-backs but small cottages on pleasant streets. There was a field by the factory where workers could play football, cricket and hockey, and gardens and playgrounds. There were schools, and after belonging to the Selly Oak parish for some years, the church of St Francis of Assisi was built in 1925. There were not and still aren't public houses in Bournville; being a Quaker family, the Cadbury family decreed that the selling of alcohol was forbidden.

In 1906 George Cadbury installed a carillon in the tower of the school. Originally it had twenty-two bells but in 1934 this was increased to forty-eight bells and four octaves, making it the largest in Britain.

Another building that claims to be the oldest building in Birmingham is Selly Manor. Although it originally stood in Selly Oak, it wasn't the manor house. It took that name when it was moved to Bournville by George Cadbury. It was a farmhouse belonging to the Smyths of Selleye and documents date it back to at least 1476. By the 1700s it was known as Selly Hill Farm. In the 1800s it was divided up into two cottages, known as the Rookery, and much of its land was built on. A hundred years later the building was badly in need of attention and it was close to being demolished. Cadbury came to the rescue and bought it. He then went through the long process of having it dismantled piece by piece and rebuilt alongside the green in Bournville. It became a museum and community centre.

King's Norton

King's Norton was another place that became swallowed up in the growth of Birmingham. Once in Worcestershire, there was a time when King's Norton was no different in size and stature to Birmingham. It was a market town and held ten fairs during the year. The parish was a large one that at one time included many outlying villages and hamlets. St Nicholas' Church dates back to the thirteenth century.

King's Norton was very much a rural area. Mills on the River Rea were used for grinding corn and the main trades and manufacturers were pottery and wool. With the coming of the canals and the railways a small industrial area did grow, mainly a paper mill and a chemical works.

On 27 October 1643 the Battle of King's Norton took place, although it was perhaps not a battle in the strict sense of the word as it has been described as more of a skirmish. Prince Rupert was on his way to join the King when he encountered Lord Willoughby, who was on his way to join the Earl of Essex's parliamentary forces. The losses were mainly on the Royalists' side, so they quickly retreated.

Two buildings came to fame in 2004 when they won the second series of the BBC's programme *Restoration*. The Saracen's Head and the Old Grammar School had been entered jointly. The Saracen's Head had been built *c.* 1492 by Humphrey Rotsey, a wool merchant, and became a public house in the eighteenth century. Although never proved, it is thought that Queen Henrietta Maria, while travelling through King's Norton in 1643, slept the night here and that room has been named the Queen's Room. The soldiers accompanying her set up camp outside.

The Old Grammar School dates back to the fifteenth century, originally as a priest's house, then becoming a school in *c.* 1550. When the new boys' school was built in the early 1900s it was no longer used.

Northfield

The ancient medieval parish of Nordfield in Worcestershire consisted of just farms and mills and included the manors of Weoley and Selly Oak. St Lawrence's Church dates back to the twelfth century, with additions being made during the following 300 years. Then, in the 1700s, a hamlet began to develop and from 1840 new houses were built in the north and the west of the parish.

In the nineteenth century nail making was the predominant concern and very much a cottage industry, but it began to decline during the latter part of the century. In the early twentieth century the work was taken over by the factories in Birmingham. However, at the same time Herbert Austin was looking for somewhere to build premises for the Austin Motor Co. Ltd. This he found in Northfield and the Longbridge plant opened in 1905.

Also looking to move out of Birmingham was Oliver Morland and F. Paul Impney. They moved their Kalamazoo paper factory here in 1913. With this expansion the whole town began to grow, with numerous houses being built.

Edgbaston

For many centuries Edgbaston was just fields and woods. The Gough-Calthorpe family owned the manor and refused any idea of redevelopment or building of factories. Calthorpe Road was just a path through a field, while Church Road, Vicarage Road and Westbourne Road were narrow lanes. In 1801 the population amounted to under a thousand but as Birmingham expanded outwards, land around Edgbaston proved to be ideal for the wealthy to build their mansions. By 1851 the population had risen to 9,269 and in 1881 to 29,951.

Charles Pye travelled through the parish on his way to Halesowen:

You proceed up Broad-street and Islington, through the five ways toll-gate; when the road inclining to the right, there is a double range of respectable houses, denominated Hagley-row, which have been erected by the opulent inhabitants of Birmingham; where they not only enjoy fresh air, but the parochial taxes of Edgbaston do not bear any proportion with those of Birmingham.

Indeed the lands hereabouts are almost exclusively the property of Lord Calthorpe, whose ancestors purchased this estate, early in the last century for £25,000, and he will not permit any manufactories to be established upon his land which tends in a great degree to make the neighbourhood respectable and genteel.

The first houses in Calthorpe's-road were erected in the year 1815; the establishment for the deaf and dumb being erected two years before. There have been within the last three years a great number of genteel houses erected by the opulent inhabitants of Birmingham, who not only enjoy fresh air, but the parochial taxes of this parish do not bear any proportion with those of Birmingham.

The church is an ancient gothic tower, the body having of late years been very much modernised, and fitted up withinside in a very neat and commodious manner.

At this toll-gate, which bears the name of Five-ways, there are now by the opening of Calthorpe's-road, six separate and distinct roads.

Thomas Anderton also wrote about Edgbaston, commenting that it:

forms a suitable, healthy, and desirable residential locality for the Birmingham upper classes. But for the existence of this well laid out neighbourhood, a very large number of its wealthiest manufacturers and professional men would doubtless reside some distance from the city – owing to facilities afforded by the railways; but Edgabaston is still a rich, well-populated suburb within very easy distance of the centre of the city.

Of the Calthorpes, he wrote that they:

were wise in their day and generation. They saw the importance of reserving Edgbaston and laying it out as an attractive, quiet suburb, and the late lord at least lived to see it covered with leasehold residences, many of them of considerable value and importance. Some of these Edgbaston houses are not only large and commodious, but are architecturally handsome and artistic.

Harborne

Harborne was a small Anglo-Saxon settlement in Staffordshire but became a pleasant, green suburb of Birmingham. Its church, St Peter's, dates back to the thirteenth century.

It was predominately a nailing community that went back to before the 1600s, when whole families worked in their cottages, but there was also an abundance of agricultural workers growing corn and potatoes. The village developed around the crossroads for Smethwick, Northfield and Birmingham and was still very much a rural community right up to the end of the nineteenth century. It wasn't until the 1930s that housing developments started to take shape.

In 1885 Harborne was described as being made up of pleasant glades and gardens. It was well-known for growing gooseberries, and the Gooseberry Growers' Society had been in existence since 1815.

Quinton

Quinton was originally in the parish of Halesowen and its church, Christchurch, was consecrated in 1841. A place of nail makers and agricultural labourers, it did also have two small coal pits.

Quinton became part of Birmingham thanks to the Rev. James Jones, who headed the parish council. Theoretically still part of Halesowen, the offer to become part of Birmingham was made in 1909 and, although many wanted to remain with Halesowen, Jones was a formidable person and, feeling that Birmingham's proposition was the best option, persuaded the town to accept the offer. Following this the town began to grow but it remained a residential area. Being downwind to Edgbaston, their wealthy neighbour had no desire to have smoke from factories descending on them from Quinton.

Handsworth

Handsworth was a small village on the borders of Birmingham, not becoming part of Birmingham until the Extension Act in 1911. In 1885 *Showell's Dictionary of Birmingham* describes Handsworth as being, 'little more than a pleasant country village, though now a well-populated suburb of Birmingham'. Indeed, until the late 1700s Handsworth was just an open area of farms, fields and heathland, with small hamlets scattered about. Hamlets with place names that still exist today as districts in the sprawling masses on the outskirts of Birmingham; places such as Birchfield, Hamstead and Perry. But in the early 1800s, with Birmingham expanding, it became a fashionable place for the wealthy people of Birmingham to live away from the increasing industry. Among them was James Watt, whose house, Heathfield House, was built around 1790. Very soon more large spacious houses were built and Handsworth became a much larger parish.

Originally known as Heathfield, Handsworth was open common land until the Enclosure Acts. Once enclosed, Watt was the first to build a house here and by 1794 owned over 40 acres, which he turned into parkland. He had his workshop in the south-east corner of the house, of which Showell writes, 'Heathfield House may be called the cradle of many scores of inventions, which, though novel when first introduced, are now but as household words in our everyday life.' In May 1874 the estate was divided up for building purposes and by 1885 other houses and streets had gradually spread around the property. Eventually the whole area was redeveloped and Heathfield House was demolished.

It was Matthew Boulton choosing to build his renowned Soho Works that changed the face of Handsworth. As *Showell's* writes:

a gradual change came o'er the scene; cultivated enclosures taking the place of the commons, enclosed in 1793; Boulton's park laid out, good roads made, water-courses cleared, and houses and mansions springing up on all sides, and so continuing on until now, when the parish (which includes Birchfield and Perry Barr, an area of 7,680 acres in all) is nearly half covered with streets and houses, churches and chapels, alms-houses and stations, shops, offices, schools, and all the other necessary adjuncts to a populous and thriving community.

Even the parish church of St Mary's became too small, so in 1894 a new parish church, St Paul's, was built in the Hamstead area to take the overspill.

Great Barr and Perry Barr

Of Barr Beacon, Charles Pye wrote, '[On] this beacon, being the property of Sir Joseph Scott, when he is at home, a very large flag is hoisted, and upon any public occasion several pieces of cannon are fired.'

Barr Beacon, a hill on the borders of Walsall and Birmingham, from which Great Barr gets its name, was the topic of an experiment in 1856. A light was ignited on Malvern beacon to see how far it could be seen and apparently it could be easily seen at Barr Beacon.

On his journey around Birmingham Pye visited Great Barr and wrote:

The hospitable mansion of Sir Joseph Scott, Bart, is surrounded by a park of a considerable extent, wherein there is the greatest variety of undulating hills and dales, woods and water together with such extensive views, as can only be found in this part of the kingdom. To this park there are three entrances, and at every avenue the worthy proprietor had erected an elegant lodge, from whence there are capacious carriage roads to the mansion. On entering the park, a circular coach drive leads to the holly wood, through which you proceed by a serpentine road nearly half a mile, when a beautiful sheet of water presents itself to view, along whose banks you pass near a mile before you arrive at the mansion. The situation of the building is low in front of the water, but being screened by rising ground and lofty trees, it must be very warm in the winter. On the left of the house, a walk leads you to the flower garden, which is laid out with great taste, containing flowers and small shrubs of the choicest and rarest kinds, together with a fountain in the centre. From hence there are delightful views, and among others over the adjacent country, Birmingham can be seen.

Also mentioned in Pye's journeys was Queslett:

There is also another lodge, at a place called the Queslet, about six miles on the road to Barr-beacon, where a spacious road conducts you for a considerable distance, by a plantation of oaks, and so through the park, wherein there are fixed numerous seats, which command delightful and comprehensive prospects. There are several that command a view of Birmingham.

★★★

And so we come to the end of our brief tour of Birmingham and its suburbs. We may not have visited all the villages and hamlets that grew around and were eventually embraced by the town of Birmingham but hopefully there is a flavour of how the district developed. Here it is once again worth remembering that some family history records may not have found their way into the Library of Birmingham's archives, so please check before you visit.